THE
ASHOVER
LIGHT RAILWAY

by
K. P. Plant

THE OAKWOOD PRESS

© The Oakwood Press and K. P. Plant 1987

First Published 1965
New Revised Edition 1987

ISBN 0 85361 350 8

Printed and bound by S & S Press, Abingdon, Oxford

*"All servants must be prompt,
civil and obliging. They must
do everything possible to carry
out the work in a proper manner.*

They must work harmoniously together."
A.L.R. Rule 14.

Jacket photograph: HUMMY at Clay Cross on 4th April 1931 with one of the regular train crews—conductor Allen, fireman Skinner and driver Banner.
Dr. J. R. Hollick

Published by
The OAKWOOD PRESS
P.O. Box 122, Headington, Oxford

Contents

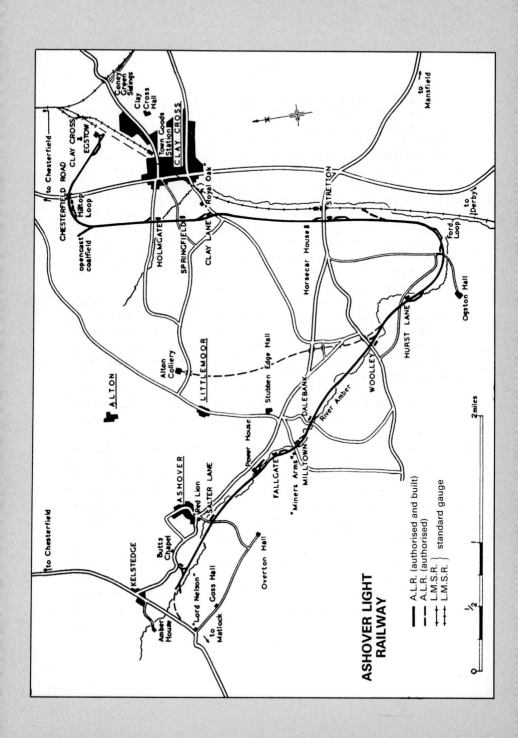

ASHOVER LIGHT
RAILWAY

——— A.L.R. (authorised and built)
– – – A.L.R. (authorised)
+—+ L.M.S.R. } standard gauge
+—+ L.M.S.R.

PREFACE

This history derives from a short duplicated account—produced jointly by Ivor Gotheridge and myself in 1955—which has been completely revised and considerably enlarged. Ivor rekindled my interest in the Ashover Light Railway and but for his determination in 1955 it is doubtful whether the present book would have ever been written. Although the 1955 publication was incomplete, until now it has remained the only *lengthy* reference to the A.L.R. Illustrated articles have appeared in the *Locomotive Magazine* (15.5.1925), *Railway Gazette* (21.8.1925) and *Railway Magazine* (10.1925 and 9.1950). Other references may be found in the *Journal of the Stephenson Locomotive Society* (2.1944), *Railway Observer* (9.1950, and others), *Railway World* (8.1953), *ABC of Narrow Gauge Railways* (W. J. K. Davies) and *Narrow Gauge Album* (P. B. Whitehouse). This list does not claim to be exhaustive.

Whilst undertaking research for this book I received considerable encouragement from the Clay Cross Company whose Director and Estate Agent, Mr. R. F. Childs, coped with my many requests and made available all A.L.R. books, maps and documents that still survive at Clay Cross. Certain items have been lost or destroyed, and apparent omissions in my story may well be due to the sketchy nature of the A.L.R. Minute Book. This results from the A.L.R. being considered as just another department by the Clay Cross Company which undertook the overall administration. Regrettably (although understandably) I have not had access to the latter's Minute Book because of its non-A.L.R. private and confidential entries. I am grateful to Mr. M. Rhodes for his diligent search at the Ministry of Transport which produced several hitherto missing items. Dimensional information is not available for Muir-Hill petrol locomotive no. 106 as the builders' pre-war records "were destroyed by enemy action," and despite extensive enquiries I have been able to discover little of the career of John May, the first Secretary and Manager.

Apart from the A.L.R. Minute Book I have consulted the A.L.R. Plans and Sections, Estimates of Expense, the three Light Railway Orders, the Ministry of Transport Inspector's Report, the A.L.R. Rules, the Annual Financial Accounts and Statistical Returns (incomplete) and A.L.R. correspondence files (incomplete). The pages of the local Press have been most helpful, especially the *Derbyshire Times* (8.2.1919, 4.2.1922, 19.7.1924, 11.4.1925, 18.8.1950, 5.3.1954, 12.3.1954, and others), and also the *Sheffield Daily Telegraph* (6.2.1919, 2.2.1922, 7.4.1925, and others), the *Sheffield Telegraph* (28.9.1951) and the *Yorkshire Telegraph & Star* (8.6.1936). I have also made use of information appearing in the *Clay Cross Company Limited Centenary Souvenir*, the *Stock Exchange Year-Book* (1932), the *Stock Exchange Official Year-Book* (1953) and *Tramway & Railway World* (10.9.1925).

A large part of this book derives from these printed sources but, as one who knew the railway only in its last few years, I have been helped immeasurably by driver Harold Skinner whose extensive knowledge of all things A.L.R. has been surpassed only by his great willingness to answer my numerous queries. Driver Bill Banner and fitter Jack Grassick have also given me hours of their time to recall much of interest. I am greatly indebted to them and also my friend, Mike Swift, who has worked most skilfully to produce an excellent set of maps and drawings. Perhaps it should be said here that the map of the Railway together with the track layouts at Clay Cross and Ashover are based on Clay Cross Company surveys, but the others are from observational sketches. The gradient profiles and station building drawings derive from photostat copies of those held by the Ministry of Transport. Blueprints, photographs and personal observation have ensured accuracy of the locomotive, wagon, and "Gloucester" carriage drawings, but lack of official material means that the "Wembley" carriage drawing *may* be slightly inaccurate.

For information, photographs and help in various ways I am also indebted to Mrs. V. Banner, Mrs. A. Broadbent, Miss V. Hind, Messrs. W. "Picker" Allen, R. W. Barnes, G. H. Buckland, J. Dunn, C. Salt and G. Towndrow (A.L.R. or Clay Cross Company employees), Miss Joan Jackson, Miss Alice Kearney (Ministry of Transport), Dr. J. R. Hollick, and Messrs. G. F. Arnott, H. D. Bowtell, J. Britton, J. W. Bush (W. Bush & Son Limited), W. A. Camwell, H. C. Casserley, C. Cathcart (Ruston & Hornsby Limited), D. Clayton, B. N. Collins, R. C. Crick, D. L. Davies, T. Davies, W. J. K. Davies, I. G. T. Duncan, M. W. Earley, R. L. Forrest (National Coal Board Opencast Executive), G. W. Green, N. F. Gurley, E. W. Hannan, A. L. Harris (F. C. Hibberd & Company Limited), T. G. Hepburn, A. J. Hills, R. G. Honychurch, A. Hurst, F. Jones, W. Jones, J. Marshall, A. J. Maund, D. Milliken (Lehane, Mackenzie & Shand Limited), G. M. Mitchell (The Ellis Travel Bureau Limited), L. W. Perkins, P. Ransome-Wallis, T. E. Rounthwaite, F. W. Sinclair (Gloucester Railway

Carriage & Wagon Company Limited), G. H. Starmer, C. R. Gordon Stuart, E. S. Tonks, A. S. Travis, R. E. Tustin, W. M. West, W. Woolhouse (Lincolnshire Coast Light Railway), J. Wrench (R. G. Odell Limited), the staff of Chesterfield Public Library, and the Reference Department of the Narrow Gauge Railway Society.

Few photographs appear to have been taken on the A.L.R. and I shall be pleased to see others not reproduced in these pages. Finally, although Messrs. Childs, Skinner and Tonks very kindly read the draft in its early stages, I must hold myself responsible for any errors and shall be grateful to anyone who can add to, or correct, my story.

K.P.P.

26 Lennox Road, SHEFFIELD 6.

I—INTRODUCTION

One of the most recent of all Britain's railways and in fact the last British narrow gauge passenger line of any length, the Ashover Light Railway arrived on the scene with the minimum of publicity, and departed without fuss twenty-five years later. Its comings and goings through the beautiful Amber valley went by largely unnoticed, for it was a local railway more concerned with mineral traffic than passengers. That the latter were carried at all was due to the insistence of the then Minister of Transport. How sharply this contrasts with the position today! When post-Great War inflation killed the standard gauge proposals, no tears were shed by narrow gauge devotees, for they knew that the A.L.R. could have had no individuality within the all-powerful Midland Railway. Even then the little railway might have been still-born, but in 1925 the day of the universally successful heavy lorry had not quite dawned.

Like many of its brethren in Ireland the Ashover Light Railway could write no success story, as for half its life it was pretty much a white elephant. That it should only shortly survive General Jackson was perhaps symbolic, for he was both creator and fond admirer. Today, "preserved" coach and "Rainbow" cafe bring back happy memories to the people of Clay Cross, but others gaze wistfully and muse on the triumphs of preservation schemes elsewhere. For if only the railway had lasted a few more years, who could say that we should not still be riding to Ashover (Butts), Ogston Reservoir or no!

Let us turn back the pages of history and see how it all came to pass.

2—EVOLUTION

Four horses snorted and stamped impatiently outside the "New Inn" on King Street. The year was 1835, and the place Derby. "Mine host" fussed around with his farewells but eventually the yellow post-chaise set off towards Duffield, taking George Stephenson and his secretary, Charles Binns, on a survey to decide the best route for the North Midland Railway between Derby and Leeds. Two years later several rich seams of coal were revealed during the excavation of Clay Cross tunnel, and Stephenson realised that mining it would be most profitable as the new railway would provide the means for its ready sale. And so in 1837 he leased several properties at Clay Cross and moved into Tapton House, a roomy mansion set in wooded country not far from the centre of Chesterfield, where he was able to supervise railway construction work and direct operations at the collieries.

The men associated with the latter venture, which traded under the style of "Geo. Stephenson & Co.", were all famous in their day as pioneers of railway construction and industrial development. George Stephenson was Chairman and his son Robert a director, together with William Jackson and S. Morton Peto (partners in the famous railway contracting firm of Peto, Brassey, Betts and Jackson), George Hudson (the "Railway King"), George Carr Glyn (a North Midland Railway director), William Claxton, E. L. Betts, Joshua Walmsley and Joseph Sandars.

A year after the Company was formed coal winding commenced at the Tupton and Clay Cross No. 1 pits, and profitably to dispose of the small coal the Ambergate Limeworks was erected at a cost of £20,000. Limestone quarried at Crich was conveyed about two miles over a metre gauge horse-worked tramway before being lowered down a lengthy self-acting incline to the Limeworks. General trading at Clay Cross commenced in 1840 and when the North Midland Railway was opened on 11th May that year it is recorded that not only did the Company supply all the locomotives with coke, but it sent a trainload of coal through to Derby into the bargain. Later in the year Clay Cross coal went by rail to Rugby from where it was taken by canal barge to London. In 1844, by abandoning canal transport, the Company became the first to send coal to the Capital by rail throughout. Business continued to expand with the decision in 1846 to erect two blast furnaces at a cost of £24,000, but the Company suffered a grievous loss two years later when George Stephenson died at the age of 67. He was succeeded as Chairman by his son Robert.

In 1851 a contract made with the London & North Western Railway to convey 60,000 tons of coal to London at a halfpenny per ton per mile was not ratified by Robert Stephenson on the grounds that it was unremunerative to the Railway of which he was Consulting Engineer. With reluctance he severed his connections with the Clay Cross Company (as "Geo. Stephenson and Co." had by then become) and his shares were acquired by Peto who, with Walmsley and Jackson, then became the sole proprietors. The manufacture of iron pipes commenced in 1864, and when a better supply of ironstone became available from Northamptonshire in 1871 the fourteen local pits were closed down. Coal production continued to increase and seven pits were sunk in the Clay Cross district between 1850 and 1881. In 1913 the firm was reconstructed as a limited Company and today it claims to be one of the largest private concerns in the country, having been owned and managed by the Jackson family ever since Sir William Jackson bought out his two partners in 1871.

When the Overton Estate, whose 1,074 acres embraced part of the parish of Ashover, came up for sale in 1918 the Company realised that it would add materially to resources if purchased, for it contained minerals of exceptional value. These included limestone (for road-making), fluor spar (used for fluxing in steel manufacture), barytes (a dressing for linen goods and a base for paints), and gritstone. Pulp stones made from the last-named mineral were a noted product of the Ashover district and were shipped abroad for papermaking purposes for many years until superseded by carborundum. Overton Hall, of which parts were built during the reign of Henry II, had been the Jessop family seat since 1872. Two notable previous residents were Sir Joseph Banks, F.R.S., the scientist and naturalist who accompanied Captain Cook on his first voyage round the World, and Dr. Bright, famed for research into the kidney disease bearing his name.

The Clay Cross Company eventually came to terms with Mrs. W. de Burgh Jessop, and the estate was purchased for £33,075. Plans were made for its development and the stage was set for the birth of the Ashover Light Railway.

3—LEGISLATION

In November 1918 the Clay Cross Company applied to the Minister of Transport for powers to construct—

Railway No. 1: a standard gauge line of about 4 miles 1 furlong 5½ chains from a point close by Stretton station (Midland Railway) to Hollow Lane, Ashover;

Railway No. 2: a 2ft. gauge branch line of about 1 mile 6 furlongs 2 chains from a junction some two miles from the commencement of *Railway No.* 1 to Alton Colliery; and

Railway No. 3: a standard gauge siding of about 1 furlong 1 chain from a point some six furlongs south of Stretton on *Railway No.* 1, and connecting with the Midland Railway.

A public inquiry into the application in accordance with the provisions of the Light Railways Acts of 1896 and 1912 was held at the Chesterfield Municipal Hall on 5th February 1919 before Light Railway Commissioners Alan D. Erskine and Captain Henry Allan Stewart. For the promoters, Mr. G. J. Talbot, K.C., stated that it was not proposed to proceed with the application for *Railway No. 3* although agreement had been reached with the Midland Railway. The primary object of *Railway No.* 1 was to open up quarries and set up lime kilns at Milltown which would provide employment for between two and three hundred men. A daily output of some 500 tons of limestone was expected (of which Clay Cross Works would take about 100 tons), together with about 100 tons of fluor spar and a certain amount of lead and gritstone. Estimates for the three railways totalled £68,712 (£47,730; £17,892; £3,090), and powers were sought to borrow half of the proposed £70,000 capital.

Standing about 600 ft. above sea level and off the main roads, Ashover village nestles in a sheltered valley below the Rattle and Fabric from which on a clear day one can see into five neighbouring counties. Two hydros and several well appointed inns provided good accommodation, and it had long been a favourite inland resort for those seeking a quiet and peaceful holiday amidst some of the most delightful scenery in Derbyshire. It had a "fixed" population of approximately 2,500 but there was a large number of visitors during the summer months; 8,000 people lived at Clay Cross and some 650 at Stretton. The promoters hoped that *Railway No.* 1 would make the district more easy of access to the general public, and that it would capture some of the milk traffic sent daily to Sheffield and elsewhere which had first to be conveyed by farm cart to Stretton L.M.S.R. station. Alton Colliery had been closed some years previously through a lack of railway facilities and the building of *Railway No.* 2, therefore, would enable it to be reopened. A daily output of some 400 tons of coal was envisaged.

The Midland Railway Company supported the application and said that some 26,000 passengers were booked annually at their Stretton station. Chesterfield Rural District Council and the four local Parish Councils were also in agreement, but Mr. H. St. John Raikes opposed on behalf of the Derbyshire County Council whose Surveyor, Mr. J. W. Horton, regarded Woolley Moor Bridge as a most dangerous place for a level crossing. Mr. Talbot told the Commissioners that the Clay Cross Company, knowing of Horton's opposition to previous level crossing proposals, had undertaken a traffic survey on 24th and 25th January 1919. On the Friday three motors and thirty-six other vehicles passed over the bridge between 7 a.m. and 7 p.m. whilst Saturday, market day in Chesterfield, could produce only two and forty-three respectively. Horton retorted that the figures proved nothing but the Commissioners obviously thought otherwise for, after an assurance that there would be no interference with the bridge structure, they granted the application, "subject to the usual safeguards being provided."

The "Ashover Light Railway Order 1919", however, was not confirmed by the Minister of Transport until 4th December 1919. It allowed the normal statutory three years for the compulsory purchase of land and four years for construction. As regards *Railway No.* 1, nine chains was to be the minimum radius of curves and 1 in 50 the maximum gradient; other restrictions were also placed on the permitted axle loads and the maximum speed which at no time was to exceed 25 m.p.h. Construction of the first six furlongs was to be undertaken by the Midland Railway, as the route lay on their property, and the A.L.R. would be charged an agreed amount. Arrangements could be made for the Midland to supply rolling stock and to lease the railway on completion.

In the event *Railway No.* 2 was not built, nor was Alton Colliery reopened. Examination of the Deposited Plans shows that the branch would have had a continuous climb to the colliery from its junction with *Railway No.* 1 west of Hurst Lane. Traffic would have been worked on the endless rope principle and, as level crossings were vetoed, extra expense would have been incurred in providing five road bridges. The Order restricted the maximum gradient on the branch to 1 in 10, the minimum radius of curves to five chains, and not surprisingly prohibited it to passenger traffic! Consulting Engineer for the A.L.R. was Lieut.-Col. H. F. Stephens, M.I.C.E., R.E.(RETD.), well known for his light railway ventures up and down the country, and whose operations for the most part were directed from his office at Tonbridge, Kent. Working with Stephens's surveyor Human on the pegging-out of ground was G. H. Wilbraham of the Clay Cross Company who later (1927) became the A.L.R. Manager. In February 1920 Stephens was asked to prepare an estimate so that the Clay Cross Company could decide whether to build the railway immediately or postpone construction in the hope of materials becoming cheaper. For 7,325 yards of single line standard gauge track including sidings and signalling at the junction with the Midland (but not for locomotives and rolling stock) the costs were estimated at £27,440.

On 12th March 1920 the Company decided to go ahead with the scheme and Stephens journeyed to Clay Cross for a discussion with General Jackson. The outcome was the submission of another set of estimates, but this time for a "60 cm. gauge line from Clay Cross Works to Milltown, 6 m. 54 chs."* The sum of £39,317 provided for estimated legal expenses, purchase of land and construction, but not for signalling and stations nor locomotives and rolling stock. At that time some 20,000 tons of Crich limestone were being conveyed the ten miles from Ambergate to Clay Cross Works by the Midland Railway. With their own railway from Clay Cross to Milltown an annual saving of £2,000 could be made in transport costs alone. The cost of "getting" at Milltown Quarry was expected to be less than at Crich, and the limestone sold would enjoy a more favourable railway rate from Clay Cross as none of the same quality was quarried so far east. Estimated annual savings of around £6,000 disregarded revenue from fluor spar, milk, general merchandise and passengers.

The Clay Cross Company was justifiably confident in the assured future of the narrow gauge railway, and in November 1921 applied to the Minister of Transport for powers to construct—

Railway No. 4: a 2 ft. gauge line of about 2 miles 6 furlongs 5 chains from a junction with Railway No. 1 some 830 ft. south-south-west of the bridge over Stretton station (Midland Railway) to Clay Cross Works.

Permission was also sought to construct Railway No. 1 to 2 ft. instead of standard gauge, its length now being quoted as 4 miles 0 furlongs

*When the railway was completed this distance was that from Clay Cross to Salter Lane.

$2\frac{1}{2}$ chains. The costs of the two proposals were estimated at £28,735 and £34,829 respectively.

At the public inquiry in Chesterfield on 1st February 1922 Ministry of Transport Inspectors A. D. Erskine, M. Kissane and K. J. M. Teasdale heard that modifications to the 1919 scheme were proposed for two reasons. In the first place there had been a change from a period of trade activity and apparent prosperity to one of depression with its attendant financial difficulties of all descriptions. Secondly, strong protests had been made by Milltown residents who were disturbed at the prospect of having a batch of modern lime kilns on the hillside between them and the quarry. After due consideration the Clay Cross Company had decided that, if an extension of the railway could be authorised through to Clay Cross, the kilns would be built there instead. A 2 ft. gauge railway from Ashover to Clay Cross could be constructed some £16,000 cheaper than one of standard gauge, and as there were already some 2 ft. gauge vehicles at Clay Cross it was planned to build to this gauge. Objections to the scheme on the grounds of danger from level crossings were made by the Derbyshire County Council (again!), the Stretton and Ashover Parish Councils, and also by Captain F. C. Schofield, assistant road manager to the Automobile Association. The inquiry was closed after some facetious discussion about whether it was better for a wagonload of manure to travel under a bridge or over a level crossing!

Before the residents of Clay Cross could raise their voices against having the lime kilns in *their* district, the project was dropped altogether! It was found that Milltown limestone had a large silica content which would have produced lime inferior in quality to that from Ambergate. There had been two small lime kilns at Milltown in Jessop's time but they were of a type which presented no dust nuisance. In fact, around 1900, there were still some fourteen small kilns within two miles of Milltown but most, including two at Ashover Butts, were disused. The two at Hockley, which can still be seen from the road between Fallgate and Ashover, continued until the stone was worked out about 1910.

A fortnight after the inquiry the Minister of Transport told the Clay Cross Company that he was prepared to make an Order provided that a service was instituted for the public conveyance of passengers and merchandise. General Jackson did not agree with the Minister's proposal that the Clay Cross passenger terminus should be where the railway crossed the Chesterfield Road for, as he told Colonel Stephens, "it would be useless making a sort of station there, which leads to nowhere, and which would pick up no passengers. The only use for carrying passengers (which would be workmen) would be from Ashover to a point at the end of the 1 in 40 gradient," the subsequent location of Clay Cross & Egstow station.

The Minister's communication suggests that the Clay Cross Company was not considering a passenger service—although this was discussed at the 1919 inquiry into *Railway No. 1*—for General Jackson could surely not have failed to appreciate the excellence of Chesterfield Road as an interchange point between road and rail. He had stated at the 1922 inquiry that Clay Cross people would be able to use the railway at Holmgate Road or Clay Lane, but he appears to have been thinking solely of workmen riding to and from Clay Cross rather than of the general public travelling to Ashover.

On 27th April 1922 Colonel Stephens submitted revised estimates to the Minister of Transport for *Railway No. 1* (£36,173), *No. 2* (£22,596) and *No. 4* (£27,391), but "The Ashover Light Railway (Extension &c) Order 1922" was not finally confirmed until 13th November 1922. Authorising construction of *Railway No. 4* it provided, *inter alia*, for the change of gauge of *Railway No. 1*, a further three years for the compulsory purchase of land and four for completion of the whole railway, a reduction of the authorised capital to £48,000, the repeal of interchange facilities with the Midland Railway at Stretton (i.e., *Railway No. 3*), and a level crossing at Stretton instead of a bridge over the railway. General Jackson had not intended that passengers should ride the last furlong into Clay Cross Works which descended on a gradient of 1 in 20 and, as the Minister was not in favour either, the length of *Railway No. 4* was reduced to 2 miles 5 furlongs 6 chains. Subject to an agreement between the A.L.R. and the Clay Cross Company dated 3rd November 1922, the *Railway* was to terminate at a junction with the Clay Cross Works (proposed) 2 ft. gauge sidings at a point some sixty-seven yards south-west of the Midland Railway tunnel entrance (the end of the proposed platform road).

To mark the opening of the railway to goods traffic a special train worked through from Clay Cross to Fallgate one sunny day in the spring of 1924. The official party travelled in clean wagons provided with wooden seats, but Thomas Hughes Jackson, Chairman of both the Clay Cross and Ashover Light Railway Companies, rode in style seated in his own armchair! Sections of the railway had been brought into use to carry rails and other construction materials directly the track was laid, and the exact date of this special train has passed by unrecorded.

It is thought that the first commercial traffic through to Clay Cross was a load of fluor spar removed from an old dump during the excavation of the cutting between Milltown and Fallgate. Previously the fluor spar had been collected by cart or steam lorry and taken to Stretton L.M.S.R. station for transhipment.

Having decided that a passenger terminus at Hollow Lane would be cramped for space and too far from the road to provide adequate facilities in Ashover, the Clay Cross Company sought powers in May 1924 to increase the authorised capital of the Ashover Light Railway Company to £51,000 and to construct—

Railway No. 5:   a 2 ft. gauge line of about 4 furlongs 3 chains from an end-on junction with *Railway No.* 1 to a point some 200 ft. west of Butts Chapel on the south side of the Matlock to Ashover road; and

Railway No. 6:   a 2 ft. gauge line of about 4 furlongs 1 chain from a junction some 400 yards from the commencement of *Railway No.* 5 to a point on Amber Lane about 400 yards north-east of the Lord Nelson Inn.

Ministry of Transport Inspector A. D. Erskine turned up once again to conduct the public inquiry in the Chesterfield Memorial Hall on 12th July 1924, and on this occasion he was assisted by Mr. T. L. Patterson. They learned that the estimated costs of the two extensions were £3,120 and £2,448 respectively, and that the prospects which were held out when the A.L.R. was projected had been more than justified. "The growth of Ashover would be considerable if afforded proper facilities" and with this aim a passenger service was to be started as soon as possible; delivery of the carriages was expected in ten to twelve weeks. *Railway No.* 6 would terminate at Amber Lane about a quarter-mile from a gritstone quarry whose entire output was then being taken away over the steeply graded Matlock road. Once the railway was built the quarry hoped to despatch by rail weekly some two hundred tons of gritstone and pulp stones. *Railway No.* 6 would also serve the Clay Cross Company's Butts Quarry which was being worked in only a small way by two men; the stone was broken by hand and as there was no weighing machine it was sold by the cubic yard. A start had already been made on the installation of electric cables for the proposed crushing and screening plant, and when fully developed the quarry would employ some sixty to seventy men and produce about a thousand tons of limestone a week.

Mrs. S. E. MacDougall, of Goss Hall, complained that the construction of *Railway No.* 6 would take away her water rights and render the land useless, but the Clay Cross Company argued otherwise and added that less than half-an-acre of land at the corner of a field was required. Mr. Erskine informed Mrs. MacDougall that she was fully protected under the Light Railways Acts and that every facility would be given to settle up the question of compensation as speedily as possible. There were no other objections and on 26th August 1924 the Minister of Transport confirmed "The Ashover Light Railway (Extension) Order 1924".

4—CONSTRUCTION

The first sods were lifted on Clay Cross Company property at Fallgate about 22nd September 1922, and a week later work began at Clay Cross. After the Light Railway Order had been confirmed in November construction proceeded apace and by mid-December was in hand at Clay Cross, Hilltop, Clay Lane, Woolley, Dale Bank, and Fallgate. In use were a steam navvy* and four steam locomotives named GUY, HUMMY, JOAN and PEGGY, which had been purchased second-hand from the War Stores Disposals Board along with rails and other equipment. Stephens planned a maximum gradient against the load of 1 in 66, but General Jackson considered that 1 in 80 would be better even though this meant heavier earthworks. "I feel that a minimum number of journeys is what we must aim at, my idea being that these locomotives which we have should be able to cope with 100 tons of material up a gradient of 1 in 80, and this would mean a minimum of about five journeys a day."

Construction of the Chesterfield Road Bridge commenced in February 1923, following an agreement with the Derbyshire County Council that the west abutment should be set back to allow for future road widening even though this meant increasing the length of the single span from 35 ft. to 45 ft. Standing 16 ft. above the road, the bridge had a width of 14 ft. 2 in. Cross girders of rolled steel joists 14 in. by 6 in. were carried on the bottom flanges of the 3 ft. 9 in. main girders, and the rails were supported by 12 in. by 6 in. timber rail bearers secured in position by angle cleats.

*This was later dumped at the back of Clay Cross locomotive shed and scrapped by Thos. W. Ward Limited a few years after the opening.

In case there was future justification for conversion to standard gauge, the formation width of the permanent way was at least 10 ft. Dirt from Clay Cross Works and material from the tip over the Midland Railway's Clay Cross tunnel were dumped to form the A.L.R.'s highest (20 ft.) embankment at Chesterfield Road which took some ten months to complete. During its construction the line of railway to Clay Cross was slightly rerouted and realigned on a gradient of 1 in 37 (instead of 1 in 40). The deepest cuttings were at Hilltop (13 ft.) and Fallgate (14 ft.), with minimum radius curves of three chains at both Clay Cross and Ashover. The track was laid throughout with 30 lb. flat bottom rails in 24 ft. lengths spiked to uncreosoted oak, fir or beech sleepers measuring 4 ft. by 6 in. by $3\frac{1}{2}$ in. There were nine sleepers per rail length spaced at 2 ft. intervals at the joints and 2 ft. 9 in. elsewhere. Colliery refuse, cinders and ashes were used in the formation of banks, and the track was ballasted with this material up to the level of the tops of the sleepers. All connections were worked by hand levers, and the design of the apparatus allowed for the points to be locked in either position by padlocks passing through bolts in the lever boxes.

The total length of bridges on the railway amounted to some 475 ft. and, in addition to the one at Chesterfield Road, included five stream openings with spans of 3 ft. 6 in. to 30 ft., ten river Amber crossings having spans of 26 ft. to 32 ft., six flood openings of two or three spans of 3 ft. to 5 ft., and one flood opening (between Ford Lane and Hurst Lane) of six 12 ft. spans. Of the river spans, seven were of the through type with 20 in. by $7\frac{1}{2}$ in. rolled steel beams at 8 ft. 1 in. centres carrying the track on cross girders with the rail bearers supported on the bottom flange. The other bridges were of the deck type, a rolled steel beam being placed under each rail with the transverse sleepers resting on a longitudinal wooden cushion piece bolted to the top flange.

Three basic types of wooden station buildings were provided, the largest (39 ft. frontage and a depth of 8 ft. 9 in.) comprising offices and shelter being at Clay Cross and Ashover. A 26 ft. by 8 ft. 7 in. version existed at Stretton, but elsewhere small shelters (13 ft. 6 in. by 8 ft. 7 in.) sufficed. All had corrugated iron roofs and rested on small concrete piles, but whereas the offices had wooden floors those of the shelters were of beaten ashes. Short rail level platforms of adequate width were provided, composed of ashes with a facing of concrete slabs. Only Clay Cross & Egstow station enjoyed electric lighting; Chesterfield Road, Hurst Lane, Dale Bank and Salter Lane had oil lamps, and the remainder gas.

Various forms of lineside fences were erected, employing six galvanised wires (the top but one being barbed) carried on wooden or iron T-section posts about 4 ft. high. Whistle and speed boards gave warning of no fewer than fifty-four level crossings—an average of seven a mile—comprising nine public footpaths with stiles, thirty private crossings and one public footpath with gates not capable of shutting across the railway, and fourteen public road and footpath crossings fitted with triangular section cattle guards and fencing. Road alterations were not necessary at level crossings except at Hurst Lane and Dale Bank where the surface was raised two feet and eighteen inches respectively.

No signalling was provided on the railway, traffic being worked by Wise's Patent Train Staff and Permit with the telephone block controlled from the office at Clay Cross & Egstow station. For this purpose the railway was divided into five sections:

A   Clay Cross to Hilltop Loop,
B   Hilltop Loop to Stretton,
C   Stretton to Hurst Lane,
D   Hurst Lane to Fallgate, and
E   Fallgate to Ashover.

Brass Staffs, engraved with the section name, had pockets at both ends, each containing three similarly engraved permits for up and down trains. Locks securing the permits were released by separate keys (one for up trains and the other for down) kept in the telephone huts, and the permits were used when two or more trains followed in succession, the Staff travelling with the driver of the last train. Sidings off the running line were also padlocked, the key being attached to the appropriate Staff and engraved with the section symbol. The telephones and Staffs were kept in locked steel huts (formerly cabs of War Department petrol-electric locomotives) at the passing loops, and in the traffic offices at Clay Cross and Ashover. Only the train conductors, who were responsible for Staff working, and ganger Skinner had access to these huts.

In July 1924 the lines authorised by the Orders of 1919 and 1922 were "gradually approaching completion" and it was expected that the final extensions from Salter Lane would take about six weeks to complete. Yet in December 1924 there were still 23 men employed on construction work, 29 less than in January the same year. The 1924 Order had been confirmed expeditiously so that passenger services might commence in the autumn, but in fact spring was fast approaching before General Jackson was able to inform the Minister of Transport that "we have completed the Ashover Light Railway."

5—INSPECTION

On 24th March 1925 the official inspection of the Ashover Light Railway was delegated by the Minister of Transport to Colonel A. H. L. Mount, R.E., and the following Tuesday morning, 31st March, he was met by John May, the A.L.R. Secretary and Manager. From the latter's point of view it was perhaps rather unfortunate that the tour commenced at Stretton for the Colonel soon noticed that gates had not been provided at the road crossing as required by the 1922 Order. He told May that all trains must come to a halt before crossing the road at no more than 5 m.p.h. In his report to the Minister he mentioned that the view at the crossing was good and "unless the County Council anticipate danger because of the density of road traffic, which did not appear to be heavy when the Inspection was made, I do not propose at present to suggest that the erection of gates is essential for public safety."

At Ford Colonel Mount carefully examined the flood opening and was alarmed to see live cinders fall from a locomotive's ashpan on to the track. He suggested that the sleepers should be secured to the longitudinal timbers by 6 in. screws instead of dogspikes, and that another board should be placed between the rails and the whole covered with ballast. A deflection of $\frac{1}{2}$ in. on the main girders as two locomotives crossed the bridge over the Amber before Hurst Lane caused the Inspector to have the earth cleared away from the buttresses, but he was satisfied when he saw there was concrete down to a good depth. Had Stephens been present he might well have suffered some discomfiture, for an error on his part had resulted in the girders being of lighter section than they should have been.

As the inspection train approached Hurst Lane, May noticed that since he had passed through the night before the points had been altered and they were going into the loop on the down line instead of the up. This made the Inspector examine the working of the points very thoroughly. He decided that the points at all crossing places should have weighted levers which would fall back to the normal position for left-hand running after a train passed through.

Level crossing gates had not been put up at Woolley although required by the 1922 Order, and Colonel Mount imposed restrictions similar to those at Stretton. He reported to the Minister that "having regard to the restricted view, I think that it would be a wise precaution to provide gates which should be fitted with discs and, if and when the line is operated after dark, with lamps. The gates should be padlocked, the key being in the possession of the conductor on the train."

Apart from thinking that clearances were a little tight near the Miners Arms Inn† the Inspector made no undue comment until the train pulled into Fallgate. He did not consider the locks on the points here good enough, and was taken aback when May told him that they were of the same pattern as those on the Welsh Highland Railway which he had previously passed as satisfactory!* But he recovered his composure over lunch at Ashover and afterwards the two men motored back to Stretton.

The train had not arrived and as it was a fine day they decided to walk on towards Clay Lane. Once again this was rather unfortunate for May, for had they waited the Inspector would probably not have noticed that hereabouts the telephone wire ran along hedges and through foliage, and was even attached to the trunks of some trees. He was alarmed to find on closer examination that the telephone wire then continued as the top wire of the lineside fence, being carried on insulators fixed to the fence posts. "While it would seem doubtful whether this form of construction afforded any saving in expense," he told the Minister, "I believe this method is a novelty, and in my opinion has undesirable features, having regard to the various ways in which communication is liable to fail owing to the position of the wire. The system was working satisfactorily when I made the inspection, but without constant maintenance I think trouble may be anticipated. A report should be called for on the working of the system after six months, so that a decision may be taken as to the necessity or otherwise for substituting an orthodox pole line for this purpose."

Colonel Stephens was present when Chesterfield Road bridge was examined and travelled with the party down to Clay Cross & Egstow. Learning that Staff working had been introduced only recently for trial purposes, the Inspector insisted that once passenger trains started running the Staff system should under no circumstances be dispensed with. His suggestion that *all* trains should be reported by telephone to Clay Cross, and not just those carrying a ticket, was not

†An old malthouse opposite the Inn was pulled down some time later.

*May had not long left the Welsh Highland! It is interesting to note that the W.H.R. Rules were used by the A.L.R. as a basis for their own.

accepted by John May who considered that the Staff alone gave adequate protection as far as the *regular* timetable was concerned.

Remembering the positioning of the telephone wire near Stretton, the Inspector thought that the Rules should allow for the possibility of a breakdown in communication, when the issue of permits would be stopped and traffic worked solely by the Staff. At his suggestion the Staffs were painted different colours as additional means of identification, but it seems that the paint wore off fairly quickly! From a safety point of view he was not in favour of the points and scotches being locked with padlocks controlled by a *single* key chained to the Staff, and the A.L.R. adopted his plan for each Staff to carry *two* keys. The first controlled a padlock on the main line points, and the second a special type of padlock fitted to the trap points or scotches which prevented release of the key when it was open. The Inspector considered that although certain bridge abutments were not all that could be desired they were sufficiently adequate. On the other hand he thought that having an additional sleeper per rail length and the adoption of somewhat broader and thicker sleepers would be worthwhile. These would minimise a tendency for the gauge to spread owing to the sleepers and fastenings being on the light side for the anticipated traffic. This same suggestion was made several times by the A.L.R. Consulting Engineer—ten years later! But it was disregarded.

The maximum speed on the railway was fixed at 15 m.p.h., reduced to 5 m.p.h. at the road crossings at Clay Lane, Ford Lane, Dale Bank, Milltown and Fallgate, and to 10 m.p.h. at the remaining cattle guard crossings. Trains descending from Ashover (Butts) to the southern point of the triangle, and from Chesterfield Road to Clay Cross & Egstow, were also restricted to 10 m.p.h.

Provided that his suggestions concerning the weighted point levers and padlocks were put into effect within three months Colonel Mount agreed to the railway being opened to passenger traffic, and this was confirmed in a telegram from the Minister of Transport the next day. John May told General Jackson that the Inspector "did not know that we proposed to run mixed trains, and he did not seem pleased with the loads I have arranged—too heavy he thought. I said the loads may be altered, but there can be no objection to mixed trains provided we work in accordance with Mixed Train Regulations. He also asked what number of carriages we propose running. I said one generally. He said no more."

6—OPERATION

The decision to commence passenger services within a week of the inspection left little time for publicity, but a notice appeared in the *Sheffield Daily Telegraph* on Friday, 3rd April, and in the *Derbyshire Times* the next day. Meanwhile on the railway all was bustle as last minute preparations were made for the grand opening ceremony on Monday, 6th April 1925.

That morning dawned anything but bright and clear. Mist in the valleys and persistent rain, however, did little to dampen enthusiasm. Chairman T. H. Jackson, despite his ninety-one years, motored over from the Manor House at Birkenhead to join the inaugural train which was headed by a flag-bedecked JOAN. All along the line the stations and halts were gaily decorated with streamers and bunting, and at Ashover the local Brass Band struck up as the train pulled into the station shortly before noon. *En route* the venerable Chairman and three ladies had in turn mounted the footplate to "drive" JOAN over "their" land. Miss Rachel Turbutt (of Ogston Hall—representing her parents), Mrs. "Dolly" Johnson (formerly of Overton Hall—representing her mother, Mrs. W. de Burgh Jessop, who was "wintering" in the south of France) and Mrs. Florence Jackson (formerly of Stubben Edge Hall—widow of John Peter Jackson, managing director of the Clay Cross Company from 1876 to 1899) each graciously accepted a gold watch to mark the occasion, whilst the Chairman was presented with two boxes of cigars.

"The great reception which Mr. T. H. Jackson . . . received . . . was an indication of the affection in which he is held as the head of what is still one of our old industrial family concerns—a concern in which there are the most intimate relations between the proprietors and everyone connected with the great undertaking down to the meanest workmen employed. In these days of great combines, or companies with no souls and no consciences, one glories to see the existence still of companies—family and industrial—like the Clay Cross Co. associated with the name of Jackson." So wrote the Editor of the *Derbyshire Times*.

Cheering from the assembled crowd heralded the arrival of PEGGY with the second special train, and the 120 guests then walked over to the County School for luncheon. In the speeches which followed, T. H. Jackson recalled that he had been Chairman of the Wirral Railway until it was taken over by the London, Midland & Scottish Railway in 1923. In fact, throughout his life he had been associated with railways, for as a young man he had gone to Canada with Robert Stephenson when the Grand Trunk Railway was promoted, and had travelled widely in both South Africa and South America before either had laid a single length of track. The Mayor of Chesterfield, Councillor W. E. Wakerley, congratulated the engineer responsible for the A.L.R. for he "had found the least objectionable way through beautiful country, and had brought lovely scenery within the reach of all without taking away one jot of its real value". Colonel Stephens, however, disclaimed this acclamation and pointed out that General Jackson had designed the railway, and all that he (Stephens) had done was to advise on certain matters. "And not always was my advice accepted!" he remarked amid laughter. Building the A.L.R. was a great achievement for the General had had no previous experience! That it was constructed entirely by Clay Cross Company employees was all the more remarkable.

On this memorable day Harry Revell was at the regulator of JOAN with Billy Towndrow as his fireman, while fitter Jack Grassick handled PEGGY with driver John Stevenson a supernumerary (because he lacked experience of the vacuum brake) and George Symonds the fireman. There were several red faces on the return journey when JOAN was shunted into the loop at Stretton, the injectors having failed! But PEGGY rose to the occasion and worked the combined train through to Clay Cross. At Ashover the same afternoon some three hundred children and adults were entertained to tea by the Company, and celebrations continued well into the night at the Red Lion Inn with members of the Brass Band in strong attendance. On the morrow public services commenced with seven trains in each direction on weekdays, eight on Saturdays, and four on Sundays. During the second week of operation, which coincided with the Easter holidays, there were over 5,000 bookings.

The original intention to have engine and carriage sheds at Ashover was abandoned after a few days experience of running, and John May applied to the Minister of Transport on 25th April for permission to build them at Fallgate instead "as that place is more convenient for the men". A site opposite the station had been selected but although the plans were approved on 8th May for some reason the sheds were never constructed.

Friday, 22nd May, saw a special train arranged by General Jackson for seventy former Clay Cross Company employees, and at Whitsun the "Fancy Dress Carnival, Dancing, Brass Band Selections and Other Attractions" at Ashover were served by ten trains, the last not being due back into Clay Cross until 11.25 p.m. The first accident on the A.L.R., albeit a minor one, occurred on Whit Tuesday. Conductor Robinson was passing from one carriage to the next "when the strap of his leather bag caught on the handle of a door and jerked him off the train. Falling against a post, he sustained an injury to his back, but was able to resume work again almost immediately."

An unusual feature of the timetable dated 7th July 1925, which was not repeated in August or subsequently, concerned the turnround at Holmgate of the 5.33 p.m. from Ashover. There was no loop at Holmgate and the train had to proceed empty to Hilltop so that the engine could run round before working back bunker first to Ashover. Two trains were required to operate the summer service, but in the winter one engine in steam was sufficient. Both regular drivers had their own engines, one duty starting at Clay Cross and the other at Ashover. Termination of the latter duty at Fallgate should there be no passengers for beyond—or working back empty from Ashover if there were—was permitted for the convenience of train crews. After being coaled and watered the engine was damped down and stood out in the open yard overnight. In the morning steam was raised by fireman Banner who lived just across the road next door to conductor Allen. Until Banner was promoted driver in 1927 the first train was driven through to Clay Cross by fitter Grassick who lived in the nearby village of Littlemoor; driver Ling (of Clay Cross) then took over for the rest of the day. Grassick worked the last train back at night only during the winter; in the summer Ling walked or cycled home from Fallgate.

The milk train leaving Ashover at 6.20 a.m. (6.30 from 1926) was introduced on 7th April 1925 although not advertised as a passenger train until four months later. Local dairy farmers would load about twenty 17-gallon churns of milk—say four at Ashover, two at Demonsdale Farm (Fallgate), eight at Fallgate, four at Milltown, and two at Hurst Lane. No special vehicles were provided, and the train generally consisted of one coach and one wagon although a loaded stone wagon would occasionally be attached at the rear. It was a proud boast that the "milk" *always* ran and made its booked connection with the

L.M.S.R. at Stretton, even when in winter a fall of snow caused a stoppage of work in the quarries and the suspension of stone trains. On these occasions locomotives would be promptly fitted with small snowploughs (kept at both Clay Cross and Fallgate) and put into traffic to ensure that the line was kept open.

The *Railway Gazette* incorrectly stated in its issue dated 21st August 1925 that "it is contemplated, if the method is not already in operation, that purely mineral traffic will be worked by gravity, as on the Festiniog Railway in Wales". But the only case of *intentional* gravity working (apart from shunting) occurred one day shortly before the A.L.R. was opened to passenger traffic when, for some unknown reason, about four loaded wagons were run singly from Milltown to Ford with a brakesman in control of each. Gravity working to Ford and closure of the railway thence to Clay Cross was rumoured about 1946, but it came to nothing. *Unintentional* gravity working, however, occurred very occasionally in the late 1940's with runaway wagons from Butts Quarry! One got as far as the old Fallgate power house before coming off the rails, and another caused a nice mess in Fallgate yard when it collided at high speed with two stationary wagons. On a later occasion frantic efforts to derail a runaway at Fallgate failed. Narrowly missing a lorry at Milltown, it fortunately had a clear run through the other crossings, demolished the gates at Woolley, and came to rest at Ford only minutes before the "Planet" locomotive arrived from Clay Cross with the empties!

Although trains ran for only nine months in 1925, they were so packed that the passenger receipts were the highest ever recorded. "General Merchandise, Coal, Lime, Milk, Artificial Manures and Farm Produce" were carried at "reasonable rates" but, because the quarries were not in full production, freight receipts were lower than anticipated.

In February 1926 Colonel Mount again visited the railway to inspect minor works carried out since the previous March. Crossing gates at both Stretton and Woolley were in position, and all the passing loops had been opened out slightly. Originally the tracks at these loops had been located at 9 ft. centres, a little too close considering that the carriages had an overall width of 8 ft.

About 1926 opportunity was taken to locate the telephone wire in a more satisfactory position, and lengths of timber about 8 ft. by 2 in. by 2 in. were nailed to the lineside fence. Copper wire was used to secure the galvanised telephone wire to the insulators, but in damp or rainy weather this had a corrosive effect and there were occasional breakdowns in communication. At road and footpath crossings a clearance in excess of 8 ft. was provided, but to avoid accidental damage the wire was later put underground at these places.

In 1926, except on Wednesdays (sometimes) and at weekends, unbalanced workings were introduced. It then became the practice to change engines when the last passenger trains of the day crossed at Stretton so that the Ashover and Clay Cross crews could retain their own engines. This meant running bunker first in one direction, generally on the trains *arriving* at Stretton. During long gaps in the service, especially around mid-day, stone trains would be worked as required with one engine probably banking from Ford. This general pattern of working continued until 1928 when the passenger service was extensively revised to allow operation by just one engine. At the same time, although retaining its passenger accommodation, the 6.30 a.m. "milk" became an unadvertised working and remained so until its withdrawal in 1930.

In the first year or two each weekday train consisted of a single carriage, but as the quarries came into full production up to four loaded stone wagons would be attached at the rear. However, at weekends and during school holidays separate stone trains were run as passenger loadings were too great to permit mixed train working. The railway's resources were taxed to the limit at Whitsun 1927, and three passenger trains in sumultaneous operation were needed to move the large crowds tempted out by the weather. But as motorbus services gradually improved so did the novelty of the railway wear off. As early as 1926 the *Derbyshire Times* had noted that an augmented train service had taken several hundreds of day-trippers to Ashover at Easter but that many more had "availed themselves of the improved bus service from Chesterfield."

One of the more remarkable aspects of the A.L.R. was its safety record, for in twenty-five years not one person was killed. There were a few accidents, of course, but none was serious. GUY was once derailed and turned over after colliding with a Clay Cross Company lorry being loaded with stone from a large stockpile at Milltown, and on another occasion there was a brush with a horse and cart at Holmgate. But on Thursday, 30th May 1930, a fatal accident seemed certain at Clay Lane. One Arthur Freeman, approaching the crossing on his motor-cycle, remained oblivious of the oncoming passenger train and ran full tilt into GUY. He was taken home by Clay Cross Company ambulance and then to Chesterfield Royal Hospital where fortunately he recovered.

Ashover Light Railway.

CLAY CROSS FEAST

(Aug 8 to 11th.).

ATHLETIC SPORTS

Wednesday, Aug. 11th.

SUNDAY, AUGUST 8th. The Train Service will be as under :

From **Clay Cross** 9-55 a.m., 2-10, 3-30, 5-25, & 7-25 p.m.
From **Stretton** at 10-18 a.m. 2-27, 3-46, 5-45 & 7-41 p.m.
From **Ashover** at 7 a.m., 12-30, 4-25, 6-25 & 8-30 p.m.

MONDAY & TUESDAY, AUG. 9th & 10th. Trains will run as under :

From **Clay Cross** at 7-45, 8-50, 10-20, 11-40 a.m., 2-40, 4-40, 5-48, 6-45 & 8-40 p.m.
From **Stretton** at 8, 9-34, 10-44 a.m., 12-2, 3-6, 4-56, 6-16, 7-11 & 8-56 p.m.
From **Ashover** at 6-30 8-38, 10-30, 11-23 a.m, 2-20, 4-5, 5-33, 7-5 & 8-30 p.m.

WEDNESDAY, AUGUST 11th.

Trains will run as above except that the last train will leave Clay Cross at 9-25 p.m. & Ashover at 9-10 p.m.

RETURN FARES. Clay Cross & Ashover, 1/- ; Stretton & Ashover, 8d.

Return Tickets will also be issued between all other stations on above dates and during the week.

TEAS and OTHER REFRESHMENTS may be

obtained at Reasonable Prices at the Popular

"WHERE THE RAINBOW ENDS" CAFE (BUTTS)

Manager's Office, Clay Cross, Aug. 5/26.   **JOHN MAY, Manager.**

JOS. SPRIGGS, ALMA PRINTING WORKS, HOLMGATE ROAD. CLAY CROSS.

On 11th March 1932 at Chesterfield County Court his action against
the Ashover Light Railway Company failed. Judge Longson remarked
that "there was a wide discrepancy in the evidence, but he had come to
the conclusion that the plaintiff had failed to discharge the onus of
putting the blame on the respondents, and therefore judgment would
be given for the latter."

By 1931 certain trains were carrying fewer passengers than were
needed to pay even the conductor's wages, and at the end of September
it was announced that after Saturday, 3rd October 1931, "the passenger
service on the Ashover Light Railway will be discontinued for the winter
season and until further notice." This decision, apparently made
personally* by General Jackson, received little publicity and rated only
a few lines in the *Derbyshire Times*. When a service of passenger
trains was resumed in 1932 for the Easter holiday period the corre-
spondent reported that "the Butts Pastures again proved a popular
resting place." But he made no mention of the railway. It was rapidly
becoming forgotten.

Nevertheless, trains ran again during Whit weekend, and on three
days a week (Wednesday, Saturday and Sunday) from then until the
first weekend in October. The timetable was so arranged that these
trains could be worked by one engine and this enabled the five Staff
sections to be reduced to three—Clay Cross to Stretton, Stretton to
Hurst Lane, and Hurst Lane to Ashover. For another four summers the
railway had a similar service to 1932 and, although the season occasionally ended in September, only the odd amendment was made to the
timings.

Although the railway was in fair shape considering its light nature
and the number of men employed, the Consulting Engineer reported
in 1934 that the permanent way would require less attention if it could
be lifted above the level of the cesses to provide better drainage. Some
short sections were attended to and the station buildings, which had
been getting rather shabby, were repainted grey. "There are, of course,
additional improvements which might be carried out if the receipts
justified the expenditure," he remarked, "but I know this is not a time
to advocate additional expenditure, but to try and maintain the line to
a degree that will in no way embarrass the moving of heavy traffic
when the revival, which we all hope is not far away, arrives."

Unfortunately, no revival came, although for the next few years
goods traffic remained steady. Passenger trains ran as advertised until

*I am informed that there is no mention in the Clay Cross Company
Minutes, and I know the A.L.R. Company Minutes are silent.

THE ASHOVER LIGHT RAILWAY.

TIME TABLE. From JUNE 6th, 1936, until further notice.
ON WEDNESDAYS, SATURDAYS and SUNDAYS ONLY.

UP TRAINS.

UP TRAINS.	WEDNESDAYS & SATURDAYS ONLY.						SUNDAY		
	a.m.	a.m.	p.m.	p.m.	p.m.	p.m.	p.m.	p.m.	p.m.
CLAY CROSS and EGSTOW dep.	7 40	9 55	12 15	2 45	4 40	7 0	2 45	5 0	7 10
CHESTERFIELD ROAD "	7 42	9 57	12 17	2 47	4 52	7 2	2 47	5 2	7 12
Holmgate (H) "	7 48	10 5	12 22	2 55	5 0	7 10	2 52	5 7	7 17
Springfield (H) "	7 49	10 6	12 24	2 56	5 1	7 11	2 53	5 8	7 18
Clay Lane (H) "	7 50	10 7	12 27	2 57	5 2	7 12	2 54	5 9	7 19
STRETTON "	7 55	10 14	12 32	3 2	5 7	7 17	2 59	5 14	7 24
Hurst Lane (H) "	8 6	10 24	12 42	3 12	5 17	7 27	3 9	5 24	7 34
Woolley "	8 8	10 27	12 46	3 15	5 20	7 30	3 12	5 27	7 37
Dale Bank (H) "	8 11	10 30	12 48	3 18	5 23	7 33	3 15	5 30	7 40
Milltown (H) "	8 14	10 38	12 51	3 21	5 26	7 36	3 18	5 33	7 43
FALLGATE "	8 21	10 40	12 58	3 28	5 33	7 39	3 25	5 40	7 46
Salter Lane (H) "	8 24	10 48	1 1	3 31	5 36	7 42	3 28	5 43	7 53
Ashover (Butts) arr.	8 27	10 46	1 4	3 34	5 39	7 45	3 31	5 46	8 0

DOWN TRAINS.

DOWN TRAINS.	WEDNESDAYS & SATURDAYS ONLY.							SUNDAY		
	a.m.	a.m.	a.m.	p.m.	p.m.	p.m.	p.m.	p.m.	p.m.	p.m.
Ashover (Butts) dep.	8 32	11 0	11 30	1 30	3 45	6 0	8 15	3 45	6 10	8 30
Salter Lane (H) "	8 35	11 2	11 32	1 32	3 47	6 2	8 17	3 47	6 12	8 32
FALLGATE "	8 41	11 8	11 38	1 38	3 53	6 11	8 23	3 53	6 18	8 38
Milltown (H) "	8 44	11 11	11 41	1 41	3 56	6 14	8 26	3 56	6 21	8 41
Dale Bank (H) "	8 47	11 14	11 44	1 44	3 59	6 17	8 29	3 59	6 24	8 44
Woolley "	8 51	11 17	11 47	1 47	4 3	6 19	8 32	4 2	6 27	8 47
Hurst Lane (H) "	8 54	11 19	11 49	1 49	4 4	6 24	8 34	4 4	6 29	8 49
STRETTON "	9 3	11 28	11 58	2 8	4 18	6 28	8 43	4 18	6 38	8 58
Clay Lane (H) "	9 13	11 38	12 8	2 8	4 23	6 38	8 53	4 23	6 43	9 6
Springfield (H) "	9 18	11 41	12 11	2 11	4 26	6 41	8 56	4 26	6 51	9 11
Holmgate (H) "	9 28	11 48	12 18	2 18	4 28	6 48	8 58	4 28	6 58	9 18
CHESTERFIELD ROAD "	9 30	11 50	12 20	2 20	4 35	6 50	9 2	4 35	7 0	9 17
CLAY CROSS and EGSTOW arr.	9 35	11 55	12 25	2 25	4 40	6 55	9 5	4 40	7 5	9 20

Note :—(H) denotes that the Trains will only stop at these Halts when required to set down passengers & pick up passengers by request.

Passengers joining trains at the Halts should be there five minutes before the time shown in time-table.

CHEAP RETURN TICKETS

CLAY CROSS, any station, and STRETTON, 6d. return. ::
Single Journey Fares at Ordinary Rates. ::

G. H. WILBRAHAM, Manager.

Jos. Spriggs & Sons, General Printers, Clay Cross.

Sunday, 13th September 1936, but the paltry receipts could be ignored
no longer and the service was suspended the next day "until further
notice". Facilities for the carriage of *public* goods and merchandise
were not withdrawn, but through lack of demand there was virtually
no traffic subsequently. For some time use of the Train Staff had been
obligatory, rather than necessary, as provision had been made for trains
to cross at Hurst Lane in most cases. It was therefore decided to dis-
continue this form of train control in favour of the "one engine in
steam" method of working.

During the next few years most of the wooden shelters at the
stations and halts were removed, and with a reduction both in personnel
and in the standard of maintenance the condition of the track gradually
deteriorated. Stripped of its glamour, the railway settled down to fulfil
the sole function *originally* envisaged—that of bringing limestone to
Clay Cross. At this time about half was sold to the L.M.S.R. as ballast.
Earlier, large quantities had gone for roadmending, and none at all
was used in the Clay Cross blast furnaces (closed in 1958) which were
supplied by the Company's Cliff Quarry at Crich.

In January 1939 the A.L.R. joined the Association of Minor
Railway Companies, formed to promote the interests of those Light
Railways not parties to the Railway Companies' Association. Its
members included several absolutely penniless concerns, and one can
well understand General Jackson's initial scepticism when approached
by the organisers. Traffic on the A.L.R. at this time amounted to
some three or four stone trains on Mondays to Fridays, with one on
Saturday mornings. BRIDGET was the working engine and JOAN
standby. In August 1939 the McLaren diesel-electric locomotive took
over these duties but persistent electrical troubles kept it out of
commission quite often.

Additional traffic was brought to the railway in 1942 when the
Mines Department of the Board of Trade took over several acres of
Mr. G. W. Astell's farm near Hilltop Loop and set up the first opencast
site in Derbyshire. Lehane, Mackenzie and Shand Limited were
awarded the contract and on 16th May 1942 began to strip the "green"
in the quest for "black diamonds" beneath. The site went into production on 6th June 1942 with one steam* and three small diesel loco-

---

*This was a standard "Wren" type 0–4–0 saddle tank built in 1918 for
the Eastburn Aerodrome at Driffield by Kerr, Stuart & Company Limited,
Stoke-on-Trent, number 3114. Latterly used by W. K. Beard of Hill Farm,
Brockamin, near Worcester, to boil pig potatoes, it was acquired for preservation
by Alan Maund in May 1959 and since restored to its original condition.

motives to shunt the fan of sidings. Most of the coal was loaded into A.L.R. wagons which were hauled by PEGGY to Clay Cross where transhipment to standard gauge wagons took place. Some 25,000 tons of coal were recovered from the Black Shale seam before the Woodthorpe Hall site was closed on 3rd October 1942. The sidings were then removed, the excavation filled in and the topsoil conserved and replaced before the contractors moved to another site a few miles away at Stonebroom.

Throughout the remainder of the War—in fact right up to the end of the railway—traffic remained fairly light, and normally one train daily of some ten wagons sufficed. After the McLaren had been taken out of service in April 1943 the Baldwins reigned supreme on the main line once again, although at any one time two of the four would most likely be out of commission at the back of Clay Cross shed. Empty wagons left Clay Cross for Milltown and Ashover about 8 a.m., but the full train was not away from Milltown much before noon. As a load of five wagons was the maximum permitted over the rising gradients beyond Ford, the rear part of the train was detached there and collected later in the afternoon by an engine running out bunker first from Clay Cross. Lack of a bogie under the bunker sometimes led to derailments on this duty, for the track was in poor condition with grass growing quite freely and many sleepers rotten or missing. The lineside fences, which had been giving trouble for more than ten years owing to the continual decay of the original posts, were mostly removed in 1943. To prevent cattle from straying, temporary fences were placed across the track where it passed from one field into another. Trains were delayed whilst the fireman moved aside the fence to let them pass, but soon afterwards some two dozen concrete-lined pits were dug out under the track and the temporary fences discarded. It had not been unknown in passenger train days for cattle to stray on to the line, particularly after dark when the headlamp was absolutely indispensable, but extra vigilance was now necessary all the time.

After 1936 there were few passenger trains. Several excursions (8d. return) ran to the Ashover Agricultural and Horticultural Show on Wednesday, 11th August 1937, and on Saturday, 8th June 1940, a train of open wagons left Clay Cross at 1.45 p.m. for Ford Lane in connection with a garden fete at Ogston Hall. Both these were occasions of note—the former saw the carriages out for the last time, and the latter was the last *public* excursion. Owing to the wartime shortage of petrol for motor-coach trips, between 1943 and 1946 members of the

Tupton Church Choir travelled to Ashover by train for their annual
Saturday afternoon outing. The last passenger train, which ran on
Sunday, 24th August 1947, was a special of four wagons (33, 13, 66
and 63) organised by the Birmingham Locomotive Club with invited
members of the Manchester Locomotive Society and the Stephenson
Locomotive Society also participating. The sun scorched down from a
cloudless sky, and so did the hot cinders from JOAN's chimney! On
the return journey from Ashover, a photographic stop at Milltown
resulted in a mass invasion of the Miners Arms Inn to moisten parched
throats. This was a day long remembered both by the landlord
("The draught's off!") and the eighty-eight passengers. For many,
it was their first sight of the railway; for all, it was their last chance to
ride it.

A month later the Clay Cross Company notified Chesterfield
Rural District Council, in connection with the Town & Country
Planning Act, 1947, that because of the high cost of operation it was
their "intention in the near future to cease working the A.L.R." and
to substitute road transport. No doubt it was hoped that the Baldwins
would last out until this could be implemented, but they were fast
becoming so run down as to be unreliable in operation. As only about
half the annual output of 30,000 tons from Butts Quarry was removed
by road it was considered reasonable and necessary in 1948 to invest
£1,725 in a new "Planet" diesel locomotive. Smaller than both AMOS
and the McLaren, it could not haul a full load to Clay Cross without
dividing at Ford. Yet it was rarely out of commission, which was
perhaps a good thing, for JOAN worked for the last time about August
1948 and then PEGGY alone was serviceable.

How much longer the railway would have lingered on is now a
matter for speculation. What is certain is that the last nail was ham-
mered in its coffin when the Railway Executive of the British Transport
Commission cancelled the standing order for ballast. Continued
production at Butts was deemed uneconomic and, although by no
means worked out, the quarry was closed down at 12 noon on 28th
January 1950. During the next two months some accumulated stocks
of stone were worked down to Clay Cross. Then, with no *raison d'etre*
left, the Ashover Light Railway was closed to all traffic on Friday,
31st March 1950.

7—THE ROUTE DESCRIBED

If we look at a map we shall see that the Ashover Light Railway operated in that part of Derbyshire which verged at one extremity on the coal mining area and at the other on the beautiful dales for which the county is so noted. The route of $7\frac{1}{4}$ miles was roughly in the shape of a letter "S" and commenced at Clay Cross Works, making the first loop of the "S" to avoid Clay Cross town. After running due south for about $2\frac{1}{2}$ miles, it turned to follow the Amber valley through to Ashover.

At Clay Cross & Egstow a large nameboard (10 ft. by 3 ft.) stood on the single low platform alongside the wooden station building. The latter comprised a shelter flanked on the Ashover side by the manager's office and on the other by what was intended to be a parcels office but which was used as a general storeroom. Close to Egstow but some three-quarters of a mile from the main road through Clay Cross, the station was an even distance in the opposite direction from Clay Cross L.M.S.R. station.* It stood almost above the L.M.S.R. Clay Cross tunnel, whose impressive northern portal was only a few yards away, an unusual situation for a railway terminus. Behind the station was an unsightly dirt tip (started in the 1930's) up which a noisy hoist periodically lifted a standard gauge wagon to tip its spoil.

The track layout at Clay Cross consisted basically of a triangle with a loop line for wagon storage up the main line. Originally there was a catchpoint on this loop but after several derailments it was removed about 1926 and replaced by an iron scotchblock padlocked to the track. That side of the triangle which was a straight extension of the main line gave access to a carriage shed and a locomotive shed, each having two roads, and terminated at a coaling stage; between the two sheds was a water column supplied from two tanks. The second side of the triangle accommodated the station while the third provided a release line and turn-round for locomotives. Wagons brought to Clay Cross were detached just short of the station and, after the locomotive (and coaches) had gone forward, were allowed to run by gravity into the sidings within the triangle. The "short straight road", a siding off the "full wagon road", was the last resting place of GUY and later BRIDGET; originally it had run through on to the main line outside the locomotive shed.

*A privilege of long standing, but not exercised for many years, permits the Chairman of the Clay Cross Company to stop here any passenger train which he wishes to board.

From the platform road the third side of the triangle made level crossings with a siding, the "full wagon road" and finally the line through to Clay Cross Works. Only the third crossing was strictly speaking on the level, for the first comprised a hinged section of track resting on *top* of the siding which had to be swung to one side before traffic could be admitted to the siding. At the second a length of track with a trestle support was removed from the "full wagon road" whenever a locomotive needed to run round the triangle. The "full wagon road" climbed away under the standard gauge dirt tip line, and loaded wagons were winched up on to a tippler. Empty wagons returned by the adjacent track after they had been transhipped into standard gauge wagons on the Clay Cross Company's goods line below. Lifted early in 1964, the latter ran to the L.M.S.R. Clay Cross Town goods station which was closed on 5th October 1963. It was worked by locomotives but, because of the steep gradient (about 1 in 20), wagons awaiting loading at the tippler could not be held by their handbrakes alone and were attached to a cable and winched down as required. Transhipment to the narrow gauge (coal especially) was effected at a siding off the dirt tip line where standard and narrow gauge tracks were adjacent, or from the bridge carrying the dirt tip line over the narrow gauge track into Clay Cross Works. The latter made a level crossing with the goods line (hinged narrow gauge track) and crossed the Works access road to reach the dust grinding plant*, huge limestone stock hopper, the limestone and slag tarmacadam plants, and Khartoum Foundry. When coal traffic on the A.L.R. diminished, loading bays were built under the siding off the dirt tip line at the former transhipment point so that tarmac could be discharged direct into lorries through the bottom doors of standard gauge wagons.

Full A.L.R. wagons for the limestone tarmacadam plant were pushed into the reception siding by a locomotive; the winch was used on a few occasions, but only on the night shift when there was no locomotive available. Narrow gauge traffic to the slag tarmacadam plant was worked with some difficulty by gravity as locomotives were too heavy to pass over a flimsy bridge originally designed to take road vehicles only. A single wagon despatched from Clay Cross loop would attain sufficient momentum to take it right through unaided. But the most careful judgement was required by the brakesman to negotiate a sharp bend near the plant, for too much braking meant a dead stop and consequent manhandling of the wagon. It is doubtful if more than a

---

*Limestone dust was used underground in the Company's collieries to assist in settling coal dust.

dozen wagons went to the plant by narrow gauge as the practice ceased after one episode when too little braking resulted in the wagon arriving in a heap!

Starting cold out of Clay Cross, trains were faced with a stiff climb at 1 in 37 for some three furlongs. The gradient eased at the end of a substantial embankment immediately before the bridge over the main Chesterfield to Derby road. A proposed "Farm Siding" to a manure dump some two-thirds of the way up the bank (0m. 24.30 chs.) was abandoned in January 1926 in favour of another some fifteen chains further on, but this was not built either. Chesterfield Road station, situated just off the west end of the bridge, was provided with a small wooden shelter and a flight of steps down to the roadway. It handled a fair amount of passenger traffic as buses running between Chesterfield and Clay Cross passed at about half-hourly intervals. During a gale in 1940 the shelter was blown over, and later parts of it and the large nameboard were used to construct a small store-shed at the back of Clay Cross locomotive shed.

Hilltop Loop, some two hundred yards beyond the station, was originally a passing place with a telephone box for Train Staff control. Latterly, when the railway was operated on the "one engine in steam" principle, it was able to store about a dozen wagons if the yard at Clay Cross was full. There was also room for two wagons in a short siding off the loop which was laid in 1926 to serve Hilltop Farm. (The set of points for this siding came from the unconstructed "Farm Siding" mentioned earlier.) Leaving the loop, the railway passed through a short cutting in a plantation at the southern end of Far Tupton Wood where one could see traces of the once numerous "bell-pits" of old ironstone workings. At the far end of the cutting, as the line turned southwards, flat open country was regained. Over to the left on a ridge appeared the houses and church spire of Clay Cross, while on the right was the opencast coal site worked during 1942. Holmgate halt, about half-a-mile distant, was provided with a siding, able to hold about six wagons, on the north side of Holmgate Road; a small wooden shelter and a telephone box lay to the south. Two halts—Springfield, and Clay Lane—came within the next quarter-mile. The former consisted of nothing more than a nameboard at a point where a footpath crossed the line, but the latter had a wooden shelter and telephone box on the north side of Clay Lane near the Royal Oak public house, about a quarter-mile from the main street in Clay Cross. Goods traffic was negligible and the main line points were removed about 1930 without a siding ever being laid. In contrast the passenger bookings at both

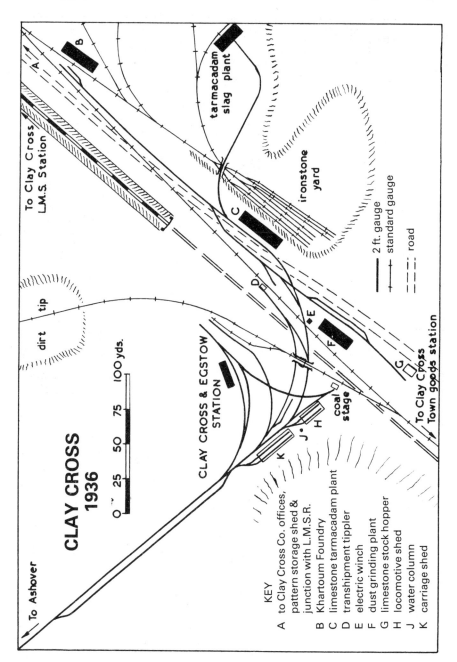

CLAY CROSS
1936

0 25 50 75 100 yds.

To Ashover

To Clay Cross
L.M.S. Station

dirt tip

tarmacadam
slag plant

ironstone
yard

CLAY CROSS & EGSTOW
STATION

coal
stage

To Clay Cross
Town goods station

2 ft. gauge
standard gauge
road

KEY

A to Clay Cross Co. offices,
   pattern storage shed &
   junction with L.M.S.R.
B Khartoum Foundry
C limestone tarmacadam plant
D transhipment tippler
E electric winch
F dust grinding plant
G limestone stock hopper
H locomotive shed
J water column
K carriage shed

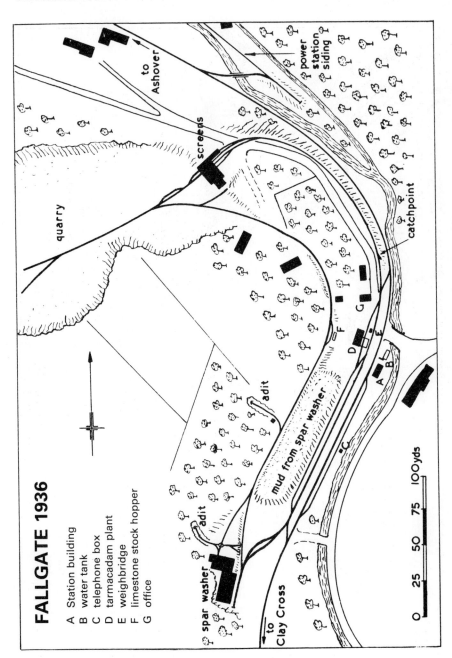

FALLGATE 1936

A Station building
B water tank
C telephone box
D tarmacadam plant
E weighbridge
F limestone stock hopper
G office

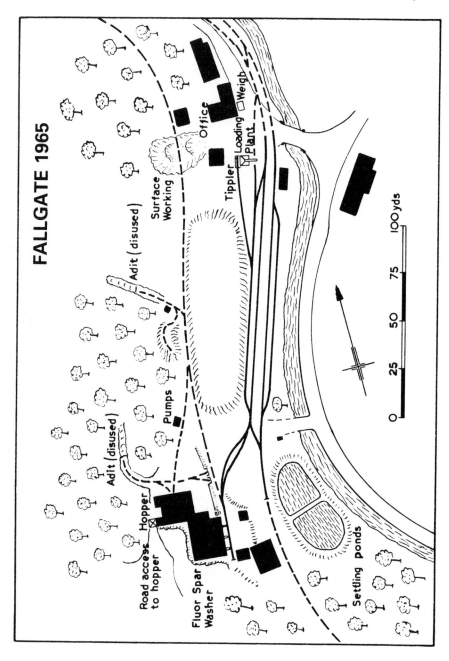

FALLGATE 1965

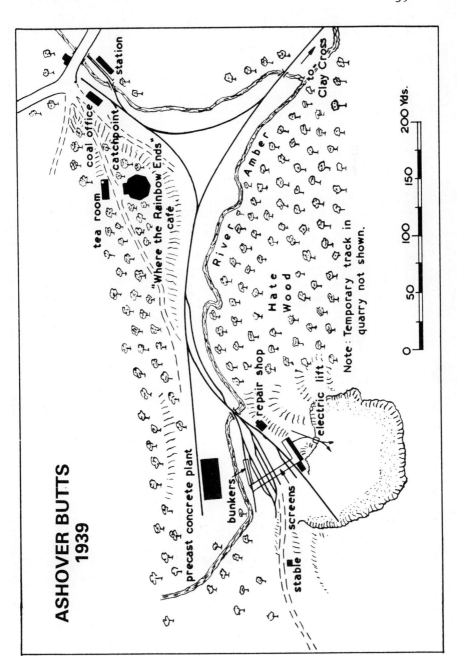

ASHOVER BUTTS
1939

station

coal office

catchpoint

tea room

"Where the Rainbow Ends"
café

River Amber

Hate Wood

to Clay Cross

precast concrete plant

bunkers

repair shop

electric lift

stable

screens

Note: Temporary track in quarry not shown.

200 Yds.

150

100

50

0

ASHOVER LIGHT RAILWAY—GRADIENT PROFILES

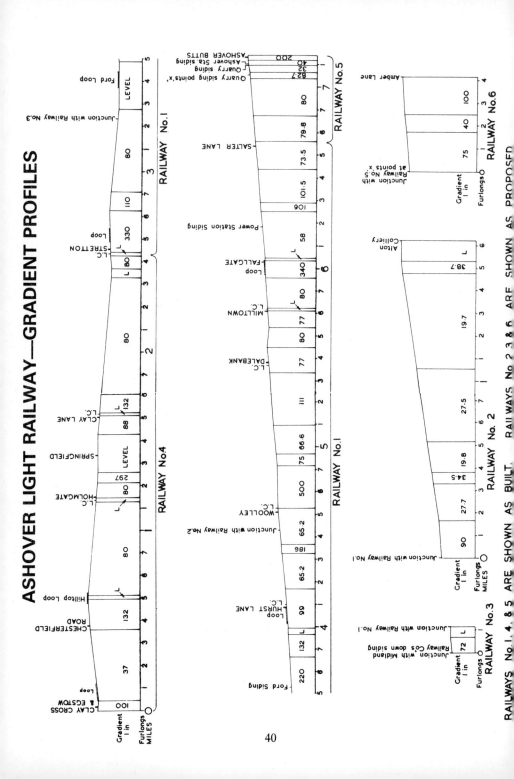

RAILWAYS No 1, 4, & 5 ARE SHOWN AS BUILT. RAILWAYS No 2, 3 & 6 ARE SHOWN AS PROPOSED.

LIGHT RAILWAYS ACT, 1896 and 1912.

ASHOVER LIGHT RAILWAY ORDER 1919.

ORDER

MADE BY THE

LIGHT RAILWAY COMMISSIONERS,

AND MODIFIED AND CONFIRMED BY THE

MINISTER OF TRANSPORT,

AUTHORISING THE CONSTRUCTION OF

A LIGHT RAILWAY IN THE PARISHES OF STRETTON OF SHIRLAND AND HIGHAM OF BRACKENFIELD AND OF ASHOVER IN THE COUNTY OF DERBY·

Presented to Parliament by Command of His Majesty.

LONDON:
PUBLISHED BY HIS MAJESTY'S STATIONERY OFFICE.

To be purchased through any Bookseller or directly from
H.M. STATIONERY OFFICE at the following addresses:
IMPERIAL HOUSE, KINGSWAY, LONDON, W.C. 2,and 28, ABINGDON STREET,LONDON,S.W. 1 ;
37, PETER STREET, MANCHESTER ; 1, ST. ANDREW'S CRESCENT, CARDIFF;
23, FORTH STREET, EDINBURGH;
or from E. PONSONBY, LTD., 116, GRAFTON STREET, DUBLIN.

1920.

[Cmd. 495]   *Price 4d. Net.*

ASHOVER LIGHT RAILWAY—STATION BUILDING

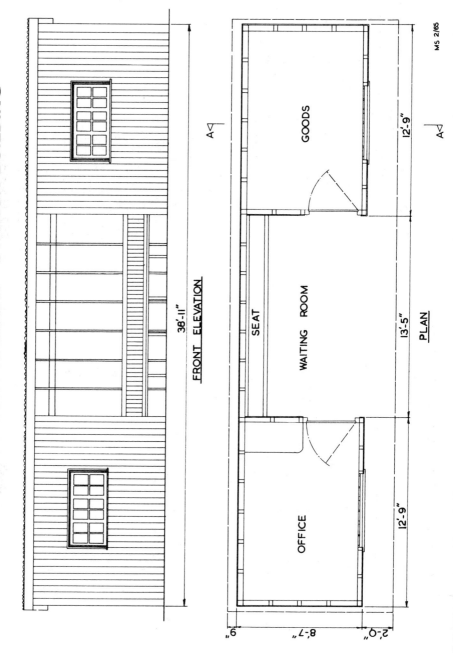

FRONT ELEVATION

36'-11"

PLAN

GOODS

WAITING ROOM

SEAT

OFFICE

12'-9"

13'-5"

12'-9"

6"

8'-7"

2'-0"

A

A

MS 2/65

43

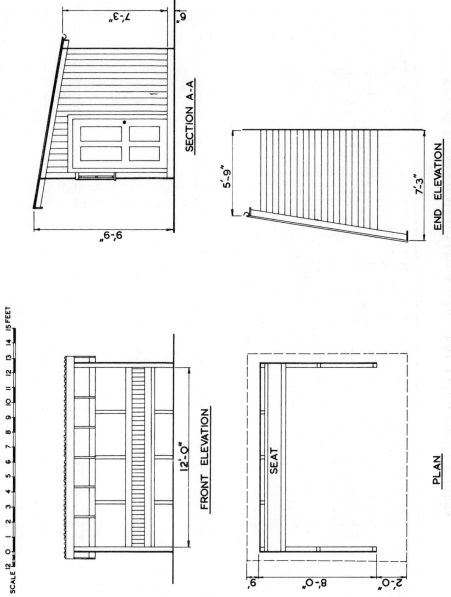

SECTION A-A

7'-3"

6"

9'-6"

END ELEVATION

5'-9"

7'-3"

FRONT ELEVATION

12'-0"

SCALE 2 O 1 2 3 4 5 6 7 8 9 10 11 12 13 14 15 FEET

PLAN

SEAT

6"

8'-0"

2'-0"

ASHOVER LIGHT RAILWAY—HALT BUILDING

Holmgate and Clay Lane were quite heavy, especially at holiday times when large numbers of excursionists would crowd the platform.

Leaving Clay Lane, the line passed through a short cutting and then set an almost straight course through flat open country. A row of trees appeared on the left, behind which emerged the main L.M.S.R. lines in a cutting from Clay Cross tunnel; the two railways then ran on parallel courses to Stretton. On the A.L.R. a 75-yard siding diverged to the left, crossed a brook, and terminated by the roadside; from here the L.M.S.R. station could be seen in the cutting a few yards away. For a year or two around 1933 when there was little demand for limestone it was stockpiled alongside this siding and later removed by lorries which did a considerable amount of damage to the track.

Stretton station, just south of the roadway, consisted of a wooden shelter and goods office, and a telephone box. Red discs were permanent fixtures on the crossing gates, and at dusk a red oil-lamp (brought out from Clay Cross) was hung on the gate on the Clay Lane side by the train conductor; he collected it later when the last train passed through. The 85-yard loop line just beyond* the low platform was used as accommodation for trains making connection with both up and down L.M.S.R. trains. When the arrival times did not coincide A.L.R. trains would sometimes wait for almost half-an-hour but latterly, when the passenger traffic consisted almost entirely of day-trippers, this arrangement was discontinued. The loop was occasionally used to divide a heavy goods train, or to stable the "Wembley" carriages which were attached to trains when large crowds boarded at Clay Lane and Holmgate. By May 1942 the southern set of points had been removed, but the loop itself was not lifted until much later.

For almost another mile the A.L.R. continued generally parallel to the L.M.S.R. before it reached Ford Loop, the lowest point on the railway. In the early days a steam locomotive would wait here ready to pilot heavy stone trains to Clay Cross, but objection was made to the weight on the bridges and subsequently the engine was attached to the rear of the train as a banker. Years later the morning stone train from Ashover would drop half its load here and collect it in the afternoon. In May 1942 the northerly set of points was removed (possibly for re-use at the opencast coal site) and as the other set had been taken out some time previously the 90-yard loop was cut off from the main line. Beyond the loop, wagons of coal (two at the most) for nearby Ogston Hall could be accommodated in a short siding which terminated

*Originally it started about twenty yards off the platform.

Plate 1: JOAN at Ashover on 6th April 1925 with the first passenger train. In the foreground are the four "drivers"—Miss Turbutt, Mrs. Jackson, Mrs. Johnson and Thomas Hughes Jackson. Driver Revell is on the footplate, with manager May in the doorway of the carriage beside bowler-hatted engineer Stephens.

Clay Cross Company Ltd.

Plate 2: Nestling in the trees on the hillside overlooking the Butts station at Ashover was the quaintly named cafe, "Where the Rainbow Ends". It is still in use, slightly modified, on the Clay Cross Company's sportsfield which lies between the Works and John Street, Egstow. *Author's Collection*

Plate 3: Two-thirds of the A.L.R. passenger stock form this crowded weekend train which awaits departure time on the longest side of the triangle at Ashover. The four Wembley carriages (handbrakes only) are marshalled between the vacuum fitted Gloucester vehicles. *Author's Collection*

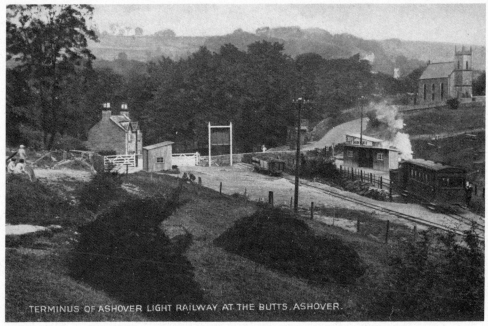

Plate 4: The Ashover terminus lay in a pleasant setting below the Butts Methodist Church. Notice the coal office (centre, left) and ice cream stall at the back of the station building. *Clay Cross Company Ltd.*

Plate 5: An early view of Ashover Butts station, probably taken in April 1925, which shows two wagons in pristine condition. Still to be built were the coal office and the short-lived ice cream stall shown in the view above.
Locomotive Publishing Co. Ltd.

Plate 6: Clay Cross, 1946. The carriage shed partly obscures the locomotive shed, and the station is just out of the picture to the left.   *W. M. West*

Plate 7: Woolley, in June 1941, showing the siding to the disused coal wharf. A platelayers' hut stands in front of the station building, and the "WHISTLE" board partly obscures a house whose occupants at one time opened and closed the level crossing gates. This section is now flooded by the Ogston Reservoir.   *J. Marshall*

Plate 8: One of the most picturesque stretches was in the vicinity of Dale Bank where the wooden shelter formerly stood on the left beyond the roadway. Notice the pit in the foreground which replaced the original wooden cattle guards. 4th March 1951. *Author*

Plate 9: Salter Lane for Ashover in 1939. The shelter has long gone but the stone edge to the platform can still be seen. *Author's Collection*

Plate 10: Chesterfield Road bridge, looking towards Clay Cross town centre on 4th March 1951. This was the major engineering work on the railway and also one of the best advertisement sites for miles around. The bridge girders were removed in September 1951, but the brick abutment on the right still exists. *Author*

Plate 11: An afternoon train from Clay Cross approaches Ford Loop in August 1932. JOAN has a light load of two Gloucester carriages. Her stovepipe chimney was replaced shortly afterwards. *M. W. Earley*

Plate 12: GUY at Clay Cross about 1934 with driver Skinner and manager Wilbraham. Notice that GUY's water-lifting gear has been removed.

Birmingham Locomotive Club "Robinson Collection"

Plate 13: JOAN at Ashover on 23rd October 1926 with driver Banner (on the footplate) and a youthful fireman Skinner. Notice the locomotive headlamp, stovepipe chimney, exhaust steam pipe running along the top of the right hand tank, short cab roof and vacuum brake equipment. The carriage lamp was not normally carried during the day. *H. C. Casserley*

Plate 14: BRIDGET at Clay Cross about 1934. Notice the full length cab roof and the water-lifting pipe running into the left hand tank. *R. G. Jarvis*

Plate 15: PEGGY shunting at Ashover about 1944 with driver Skinner. Notice the cab back-sheet cannibalised from the second GUY and its tell-tale hole between the spectacles; this had carried a pipe from the rear dome to the vacuum ejector. The water-lifting gear running from the rear of the left hand tank was not in use and the water hose hanging over the rear of the bunker was there in case of emergency. Notice also the small hand-lamp over the smoke-box. *P. Ransome-Wallis*

Plate 16: HUMMY leaving Stretton on 26th August 1937 with a loaded stone train for Clay Cross. Wagons 10, 13, 49 and 7. Fireman Allen (cloth cap) and driver Skinner. *W. A. Camwell*

Plate 17: JOAN pauses at Stretton on 24th August 1947 with the last passenger train, a special organised by the Birmingham Locomotive Club. Note the lifting jack on the buffer beam and the 8-link coupling set above it. *W. A. Camwell*

Plate 18: Clay Cross, 25th July 1934, showing one Gloucester and one Wembley carriage. The Clay Cross blast furnaces are in the right background.

Dr. J. R. Hollick

Plate 19: Fallgate yard, looking towards Ashover, in 1946. *W. M. West*

Plate 20: Derelict in Clay Cross yard on 4th March 1951 was the wagon converted to carry the large 9-ton tar-tank to and from Fallgate tarmacadam plant. *Author*

Plate 21: The former Leek & Manifold transporter wagon out of use at Ford Loop in June 1941, not long before its removal to Clay Cross for scrap. Behind it is one of the eight rapidly deteriorating Wembley carriages also in store here at the time. *J. Marshall*

Plate 22: One of the Wembley carriages in open storage at Ford Loop in June 1941. The side nearest to the camera was completely open but the upper section of the other was enclosed by wire netting. *J. Marshall*

Plate 23: Gloucester carriage No. 1 before fitting of the lamp brackets and steam heating pipes. *Official photograph*

Plate 24: PEGGY approaches Ashover about 1944 with coal for the boiler at the concrete plant and empties for the quarry. The leading wagon, 69, is one of the few having sides of which only the centre section could be unpinned. Wagons of coal for Ford siding and the wharves at Woolley and Ashover were always propelled from the previous loop as in each case the points were facing from the Clay Cross direction. *P. Ransome-Wallis*

Plate 25: JOAN on the reversing triangle at Clay Cross, showing the "level" crossing referred to on page 34. The wagons are standing on the trestle support which carried the "full wagon road". *Locomotive & General Railway Photographs*

Plate 26: JOAN derailed near Dale Bank with a loaded stone train after hitting an obstruction on the track.   *Author's Collection*

Plate 27: The worn out crushing and screening plant at Butts Quarry on 7th April 1950, looking towards Clay Cross. Piles of screenings cover disused and lifted tracks.   *Author*

Plate 28: Petrol-electric locomotive AMOS at Fallgate tarmacadam plant on 9th
June 1943.   *L. W. Perkins*

Plate 29: No shed was provided for the "Planet" diesel locomotive which stood
out in the open at Fallgate. Its cab could be entered from the right hand side only.
7th April 1950.   *Author*

Plate 30: Brought in by contractors Marple & Gillott Limited to assist with track-lifting, this small "Planet" diesel locomotive watched the A.L.R. "Planet" work most of the demolition trains. Fallgate, 4th March 1951.   *Author*

Plate 31: The McLaren diesel-electric locomotive at Fallgate with cab controller very prominent.   *R. E. Tustin*

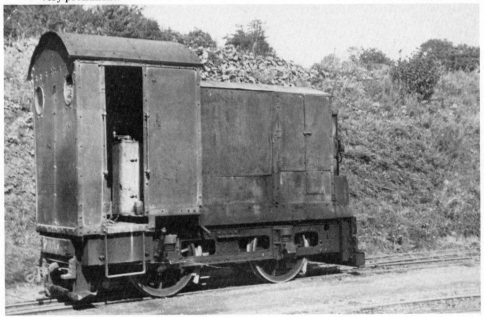

Plate 32: Some seventeen years after it worked at the opencast sidings near Hilltop Loop, Kerr Stuart 3114 was acquired for preservation by Alan Maund. Seen here at Church Cottage, Hindlip, near Worcester, in 1962, it is currently located at the Narrow Gauge Railway Centre of North Wales at Gloddfa Ganol, near Blaenau Ffestiniog. *A. J. Maund*

Plate 33: "Muir Hill Fordson Locomotive No. 106" looks home-made, yet it was built in Manchester; Fallgate, 9th June 1943. *L. W. Perkins*

alongside Ford Lane. No halt was provided here although passengers were occasionally picked up unofficially. Beyond lay the picturesque Amber valley through which the line threaded its way on a gradient of 1 in 220 to reach Hurst Lane halt where the wooden shelter and telephone box stood at the far end of the 140-yard loop adjacent to the ungated road crossing. A "sausage" water tank on wooden trestles was provided with two hoses between the tracks so that engines of up and down trains could take water simultaneously. Until about 1930 there was a set of points by the shelter but no siding was ever laid. The loop and the water tank were still here in May 1942, but were removed shortly afterwards.

The gradient now steepened to 1 in 99 and leaving behind the wooded slopes the railway ran through open country to reach Woolley. Here there was the usual shelter, together with a telephone box, platelayers' cabin, Clay Cross Company coal office (closed about 1934) and a siding to hold four or five wagons. The telephone was moved from the box to the office as coal sales were very good at first, but they soon tailed off. About 1930 the telephone box was taken to a point mid-way between Stretton and Ford where it housed a pump installed when the water supply for cattle was cut off with the building of the railway. Red discs were permanently affixed to the level crossing gates; in addition, at dusk and during foggy weather, a red oil-lamp, locked in the telephone hut (or office) when not in use, was hung on the gate on the Dale Bank side by the train conductor. Originally it was the conductor's job to open and shut the gates. Later this was attended to by the occupants of a large stone house by the crossing in return for a free lineside garden plot, but in the last few years it reverted to the train crew.

Beyond Woolley the trees came down almost to the side of the line which crossed the Amber twice as it climbed through the wide valley to Dale Bank halt*, where the wooden shelter produced few passengers ever. A quarter-mile further on the railway crossed a small bridge and came to Milltown halt. The wooden shelter here was approached by a short roadway from Oakstedge Lane, just to the south of another bridge over the Amber. A set of points was removed about 1930 without a siding being added.

*Less than half-a-mile up the hill to the right was Stubben Edge Hall, purchased from Frederick Arkwright in 1873 by Sir William Jackson for his son, John Peter Jackson. It was taken over about 1922 by the Sheffield Works Convalescent Association, and since 1962 has been the residence of David Kenning.

As the gradient eased the railway crossed the road, passed the Miners Arms Inn on the left and turned northwards into a short deep cutting beyond which stood a fluor spar washing plant with its attendant sidings. One of these climbed into the Clay Cross Company's limestone quarry* and two others penetrated narrow crevices before plunging into the hillside to the fluor spar mines. The earlier lead miners here were not interested in fluor spar which they cast aside as refuse, and so the Clay Cross Company was able to obtain it initially merely by surface digging. In fact, a little fluor spar gravel is still worked today although the main source is rock from the mines. Minerals from the Top Log Mine were conveyed to the spar washer by an aerial ropeway which employed two 300-yard winding ropes from the Clay Cross Company's colliery at Morton. The ropeway was erected in 1941 but ran for only three or four years.

Fallgate station, with its wooden shelter flanked by a telephone box and a "sausage" water tank, stood at the north end of a 100-yard loop adjacent to the level crossing. A coal sales depot was installed by the Clay Cross Company in 1925, and two years later a limestone dust grinding plant was built. Repeated complaints from local residents, however, led to the latter being taken down in 1930 and re-erected at Clay Cross Works. A tarmacadam plant built in 1936 lasted some twelve years before being dismantled by W. Bush & Son Limited of Alfreton, even though the quality of tarmacadam produced was not good. (Apparently the limestone was not sufficiently absorbent to take the correct quantity of tar.) At the north end of the yard a horse-worked track ran through a catchpoint and then banked away steeply on a gradient of 1 in 13 to a set of screens and loading hoppers which were fed from a high level line out of the quarry. Many thousands of tons of limestone were removed before production ceased in 1936; the quarry reopened temporarily in 1942 but was finally closed down in 1946.

Leaving Fallgate the main line turned north-west to be hemmed in on one side by a moss-covered wall and on the other by trees which overhung the rippling Amber. As the gradient steepened to 1 in 58 Fallgate power house, with its stone walls and red asbestos roof, came into view on the opposite bank close by an old mill and waterwheel. The power house was built by the Clay Cross Company at the same

*Although much nearer to Fallgate station it was always referred to as *Milltown* Quarry, and the same applied to the washing plant. Nowadays, to confuse things still further, the fluor spar workings are known as *Overton* Quarry!

time as the A.L.R. to provide electricity for the quarries, although provision was made for private residents in Ashover for a short time until the village was connected to the public supply. Coal for the power house "Lancashire" boiler naturally went in by rail, but a double reversal was necessary as the main line points were trailing from Clay Cross; the shunting neck was able to accommodate a locomotive and one wagon only. Relief driver Grassick once shot over the bridge with a train from Ashover and ran into the bank, but this was unintentional for the main line points had stuck in the wrong position! Although the siding is mentioned in Colonel Mount's Inspection Report, it is surprising that the Minister of Transport placed no prohibition on locomotives crossing the bridge, for it was of faulty construction. Somehow the girders had been set at well over 2 ft. centres with the result that the entire weight of trains was taken by the wooden sleepers! Erection of an overhead power line from Clay Cross Works about 1927 enabled the power house to be closed down, and thereafter the siding was used only on the infrequent occasions when fluor spar was ground at the old mill. By this time it was considered unsafe for a locomotive to cross the bridge owing to the unsound condition of the sleepers, and wagons were pushed over it by hand. Although both siding and bridge were removed about 1941, the power house remained and it is now rented from the Clay Cross Company by the tenant of Demonsdale Farm to house a multitude of battery hens.

The main line kept to the floor of the gradually narrowing valley and as the Amber became more sinuous bridges carried the track first from one side and then to the other. Up on the hillside the main road reached Ashover and from alongside the Red Lion Inn a steep and picturesque lane descended; where it crossed the railway stood a small wooden shelter with nameboard, "Salter Lane for Ashover". The lane is the Hollow Lane mentioned in the 1919 Light Railway Order, and its continuation past a set of stone horse-mounting steps is known as Salter Lane. Less than half-a-mile away over the hill it reached Overton Hall which has been put to several uses* since purchased by the Clay Cross Company in 1918.

The railway continued at 1 in 80 for another half-mile and skirted

*A Major Benthall lived here from 1920 to 1928 and it was in use as a Youth Hostel from 1933 to 1940 and again from 1949 to 1956; the Borough of Derby rented it from 1940 to 1942 as a school and then Derbyshire County Council had it for an approved school from 1942 to 1948. As the Youth Hostellers moved out in 1956 the Old People moved in and it was their Home until re-let in 1962 as a Country Hotel.

"The Butts"—a large open space at the head of the valley—before
running into the terminus at Ashover (Butts). This was situated some
distance out of the village at a point where the road turned extremely
sharply before climbing away steeply in both directions. The Deposited
Plans show that the station was originally intended to be much nearer
to the Butts Methodist Church, still on the south side of the road but
away from the rather awkward bend. To have achieved this, however,
a substantial realignment would have been necessary owing to the
difference in levels. Hereabouts the Clay Cross Company had considered building a large number of quarrymen's houses, but they were
not found to be necessary.

The track layout at Ashover, in which connections from the Clay
Cross Company's Butts Quarry formed a triangle with the line to the
station as its base, avoided the need for a turntable. Weekend excursion
trains terminated on the longest side of the triangle which continued
for some distance before a loop (the "quarry full road") diverged to the
left. (A catchpoint between the triangle and the loop was never put in
although Colonel Mount had suggested that one be provided.) The main
line here was the "quarry empty road" and from it a siding ran through
to the pre-cast concrete plant which was built in 1934; it employed
several women (and later a few German prisoners-of-war) until it
closed in 1947. Crossing the Amber by a sturdy stone bridge which
had carried a cart track before the railway was built, the main line
passed a small repair shop and office as it ran into Butts Quarry.

The station platform at Butts commenced just off the end of a
tiny bridge and passengers were protected from falling into the stream
by a wire fence. The station building was very similar to the one at
Clay Cross and had a wooden shelter flanked on either side by a small
office. Sweets and confectionery were sold for a short time from the
office nearest the roadway, after which it stood empty for many years;
latterly moulds for some of the smaller items made at the Butts concrete
plant were stored there. The other office housed the telephone and was
used for Staff control purposes only. Across the stream was a small
goods yard and Clay Cross Company coal wharf which was served by a
siding (with catchpoint) running up to the low stone wall alongside the
road.

At the back of the station building Jack Holmes set up an ice cream
stall which did good business during 1925, but closed down a year later
owing to competition from the A.L.R.'s own cafe. Of octagonal shape,
this was situated across the stream on a wooded slope overlooking

the station and was opened in time to catch the summer traffic of 1926. John May thought up the unusual name of "Where The Rainbow Ends" and arranged for the crockery and cutlery to be inscribed "A.L.R." A net profit of £36 was made the first year on a turnover of some £280, and the nominal takeover by the Clay Cross Company on 1st January 1927 was possibly done to avoid the preparation of detailed statistical returns to the Ministry of Transport. Jack Broadbent was appointed manager in 1927 in succession to Mabel Holmes (wife of Butts Quarry foreman Hedley Holmes, but no relation of Jack Holmes) who took over the running of the coal wharf. Tea and minerals were served in a small outhouse at busy periods for the "Rainbow" cafe soon became a popular rendezvous with both diners and summer dancers who were provided with late excursion trains. During the winter months from 1932 to 1940 the building was hired out to the Derbyshire County Council as a domestic subjects classroom, and for the next four years it served as a school for evacuee children of many nationalities living at Amber House, Kelstedge. Last used as a cafe proper in September 1939, the "Rainbow" was dismantled during the summer of 1950 and re-erected the next year on the new sportsfield at Clay Cross. A small metal plaque commemorates its reopening by Roland Jackson on 24th May 1952.

In passenger days single coach trains ran into Butts station to unload and waited there until departure time. Then, because there was no run-round loop, they reversed towards the quarry before setting forward towards Salter Lane. If two or three empty wagons were attached at the rear a similar procedure was followed, except that a reversal was made directly all passengers had detrained; the wagons were then propelled into the "quarry empty road" or, if the way was clear, right through to the quarry screens. Such wagons waiting in the "quarry full road" would be coupled up and the train would wait time on the longest side of the triangle. (This occasionally gave rise to complaints from intending passengers who, waiting unsuspecting on the station platform, realised too late that the train was leaving without them!) Longer mixed trains meant that the engine and coach had to run round the triangle before propelling the wagons towards the quarry. But after suspension of the passenger service the engine would work its train into the "quarry empty road" and reverse through the "quarry full road", propelling the full wagons to the longest side of the triangle; the engine would then run round before proceeding towards Clay Cross.

Some fifteen to twenty small four-wheel wooden tubs were in use latterly at Butts Quarry for carrying stone. They were propelled by hand over a fanwork of temporary 2 ft. gauge tracks not connected to the main line which led from the various quarry working faces to an electric lift having a safe load of three tons. After being weighed the tubs were tipped, and the stone proceeded through the crusher and screens before being loaded into wagons standing below. There was a set of storage hoppers beyond the screens but, when output was considerably greater than demand, stone was stockpiled alongside the turning triangle—at times so close to the running rails as to foul the footboards of carriages being shunted—and loaded mechanically into wagons as required. As the locomotives had insufficient clearance to pass under the screens, a horse was used for shunting the yard; it was mostly employed on clearing wagons from the "quarry empty road". One siding ran direct to the quarry face and was used to bring out large stone or "pitchings". Another beyond the screens stored empty wagons and, as Amber Lane was not reached as originally planned, it was in fact the most westerly point on the Ashover Light Railway.

8—LOCOMOTIVES AND ROLLING STOCK

(a) STEAM LOCOMOTIVES

By the time the First World War was over, among the locomotives of various types which had seen service with the War Department during the campaign in France, there were many 4–6–0 pannier tanks built by the Baldwin Locomotive Works at Philadelphia, U.S.A. In 1922 several were included in a sale of surplus equipment thought to have been held at Darlington. General Jackson offered £1,000 for four of them, but the War Stores Disposals Board regarded this sum as totally unacceptable. Shortly afterwards, however, they wrote to say that as nobody else had shown interest the locomotives were his if he still wanted them! Prospective buyers may well have anticipated difficulty in getting spares from America and, although offered for sale comparatively cheaply, only eleven of this Baldwin type subsequently worked in Britain. The A.L.R. eventually had six, the Snailbeach District Railways two, and there was one each with the Glyn Valley Tramway, Welsh Highland Railway, and Rainham cement works of the British Standard Cement Company Limited.

General Jackson's four purchases were delivered by rail to Clay Cross Works and put in the pattern storage shed. One by one they were overhauled and tested on a 100-yard length of temporary track laid inside a standard gauge siding running towards the Clay Cross Company offices. Then they went out to help with A.L.R. construction work, the first being used at Clay Cross and the others respectively at Fallgate, Clay Lane and Clay Cross. At this time they still retained their old War Department numberplates on the tank sides, but these were replaced during 1924 by brass nameplates cast in the foundry at Clay Cross Works and using the same bolt-holes. The names selected – HUMMY, GUY, JOAN and PEGGY – had some significance as they were those of General Jackson's children.

By the time the railway was completed all four locomotives were somewhat run down. As GUY was not expected to work again, two further locomotives of the same type were obtained for £300 each from Thos. W. Ward Limited of Sheffield, and these arrived at Clay Cross about April 1925 (though not taken into stock until 1926). Both were in quite good condition and no overhaul was necessary but, as the width of the tyre treads was an inch less than those on the first four engines, wider tyres were fitted to the centre wheels to avoid derailments. One was then named BRIDGET and the other received the nameplates from GUY. Fitter Grassick discounts the version which gives HUMMY as the one involved, for he made the change of nameplates.

JOAN, PEGGY and the second GUY were the only ones to carry the letters "A.L.R." on the cab sides (red, blocked yellow); they were painted Midland "red"* with yellow and black lining by the Clay Cross Works wagon repair shops painters, but the others received an unlined black livery from the A.L.R. staff. Latterly black became standard for all six.

The dimensions of these locomotives (Baldwin class 10–12–D13) were:

Cylinders: 9 in. by 12 in.	Heating Surface (tubes): 231 sq. ft.
Coupled Wheels (dia.): 1 ft. 11½ in.	Heating Surface (firebox): 23½ sq. ft.
Bogie Wheels (dia.): 1 ft. 4 in.	Grate Area: 5½ sq. ft.
Boiler diameter: 2 ft. 9 in.	Boiler Pressure: 178 lbs./sq. in.
Boiler length: 19 ft. 6⅛ in.	Coal Capacity (bunker): 15½ cwts.
Firebox length: 2 ft. 7⅜ in.	Water Capacity: 396 gallons
Firebox width: 2 ft. 3½ in.	Weight (empty): 10 tons 15 cwts.
Tubes (brass): 83 of 1½ in. dia.	Weight (loaded): 13 tons 15 cwts.
	(approx.)

Tractive Effort @ 75% of Boiler Pressure 5,510 lbs.

*It was actually more a crimson lake (or maroon) than red.

These locomotives had copper fireboxes and brass tubes, with the bar frames and two domes giving them a typical American appearance. In 1925, before passenger services started, an acetylene headlamp was substituted for the less effective oil-lamp on the top of the smokebox. The leading dome held sand for the front wheel sanders and the steam dome was surmounted by two pop safety valves and a whistle. Square-cased slide valves over the two outside cylinders were actuated by Walschaerts valve gear. Coal was kept both in the bunker and on the footplate, although occasionally large lumps were stacked on top of the boiler. The flat-topped pannier tanks stopped short of the cab which originally was not enclosed at the rear. Both steam- and hand-brakes were standard on this type of locomotive, but the A.L.R. examples were modified at Clay Cross for working passenger trains and equipped with combined steam and vacuum brake ejectors. These and the necessary piping for the right hand side of the locomotive were supplied by the Consolidated Brake & Engineering Company Limited (after some delay in obtaining locomotive drawings from America!) and fitted in January 1925. No spare ejectors were purchased and after the last two engines arrived the equipment was switched around as required; in the last few years before closure it was removed.

The two small sandboxes under the cab floor were not entirely satisfactory, as water found its way in when the footplate was hosed down. In addition, with the pipes to the rear wheels inevitably fracturing in the event of a derailment, rear sanding was abandoned quite early on and the cab sandboxes were used to hold cotton waste. To minimise damage to the front sand pipes a short length of rubber hose was fitted to each. On damp or rainy days liberal sanding was necessary, and one or other of the pipes was blanked off to prevent all the sand being used on one trip.

On one or two occasions before the passenger service started drivers were obliged to lift water from the river at Hurst Lane (and once at Holmgate) because the water in the tank at Hurst Lane was then dirty and unreliable. The gear, which was on the left-hand side of the locomotive, was little used subsequently and, even though JOAN was so fitted to the end, it was removed from both HUMMY and BRIDGET, and possibly PEGGY too. As the hinges on the tank filler–hole lids broke off they were not replaced. Instead, new and heavier lids, fashioned from thick steel plate with three securing pegs, were fitted.

In early photographs of these locomotives a pipe can be seen running above the right hand tank to the smokebox. This carried exhaust steam from the vacuum ejector, but condensation in the smokebox meant that each time the ejector was opened a shower of black smuts descended on all and sundry. An effective cure was obtained by shortening and repositioning the pipe so that it discharged steam above the cab roof and condensate through a small drain pipe.

During A.L.R. construction work the Baldwins were found shy for steam, and in the next few years fitter Grassick embarked on a series of experiments and modifications to cure this failing. The original brass tubes were replaced quite early on by steel tubes with brazed copper ends at the firebox end. Although the firebox heating surface was adequate there could be no depth to the fire because of the closeness to the bottom of the firebox of the lowest set of tubes. To provide some, the normal flat-top firebars were replaced by ones of concave shape made specially at Clay Cross Works. Unfortunately these burned through on the bend at each side after only three or four days use, and although the design was altered this difficulty was not overcome and the normal firebars were replaced.

Alterations were then made to the ashpan which originally had hinged flaps at the front and rear. The lower side-plates of the new ashpan were made to slope outwards and the bottom plate to slope to one end. A much better draught to the fire and a cleaner ashpan resulted. So that the smokebox could be emptied of ashes more easily the bottom was bricked in with one layer of firebricks and fireclay just clear of the tubes and washout plugs.

Several extensions to the blastpipe were tried out until one with a satisfactory inside diameter was found. Fitting a "crossbar" to split the blast was not successful for it made the blast so keen as to lift many cinders from the fire. The "crossbar" was removed, although passengers who suffered scorched trousers on the 1947 excursion train may find this hard to believe! Final modifications to the steaming arrangements were made about 1932 when the sheet steel stovepipes were replaced by cast iron capped chimneys three inches less in height but about an inch and a half wider in the bore.

Although certain spare parts were purchased out (e.g. tyres), many—including the new chimneys—were made at Clay Cross Works. The Welsh Highland Railway, which had one similar Baldwin locomotive, took full advantage of this "service" in the 1930's through Colonel Stephens, and obtained on various occasions valve gear parts, axlebox covers and other small items.

Provided the tubes were kept well cleaned—normally half were cleaned one morning and the remainder the next—the modified Baldwins were never short of steam. Owing to the abrupt changes in gradient at Hilltop and Ford firing was a difficult job, and much coal was ejected unburned from the chimney when working hard. The A.L.R. was not an easy road but, despite a minimum of maintenance, the Baldwins managed to struggle through the Second World War and PEGGY had the satisfaction of outliving all others of the type in this country.

It is difficult to arrive at a definite conclusion concerning the names and numbers for the nameplates and other parts were changed around several times during repairs and overhauls. A close scrutiny of the motion of the engines revealed Baldwin serial numbers which did not in any way agree with the Baldwin works numbers, and this confirms reports that during the War in France damaged and run-down locomotives were cannibalized for spare parts. The table below gives the position as far as it is known, even though at times this might seem to conflict with the text.

Name	No. (a)	Building Date	W.D. No.	Baldwin plate on delivery to A.L.R.	Baldwin plate in August 1925	Final Baldwin plate
HUMMY	64	1. 3.1917	645	45227 (b)	45227	44370 (c)
GUY (first)	—	1.11.1916	525	44370 (b)	44737	45227
JOAN	61	1. 1.1917	815	44720	44720	44720
PEGGY	60	1. 1.1917	838	44743 (b)	44743	44743
GUY (second)	63	1. 1.1917	790	44695	44695	44695
BRIDGET	62	1.11.1916	832	44737	44370	44737 (d)

(a) Small plates carried outside the cab showed the boiler number allotted for insurance purposes. The table shows the position at 3rd August 1943.

(b) As recorded by the A.L.R. in August 1924.

(c) One of the two worksplates carrying this number is on display in the Narrow Gauge Museum at Towyn, Merionethshire.

(d) One of the two worksplates carrying this number is on display in the Clay Cross Company offices (with GUY nameplate).

Individual notes on the locomotives are as under.

HUMMY—named after Lt.-Col. Henry Humphrey Jackson, the present Chairman and joint managing director of the Clay Cross Company; fitted with brass nameplates measuring 23 in. by 7 in. with letters 5¾ in. high on a red background. The first engine to be overhauled, it was driven up to the A.L.R. yard on temporary lengths of track and assisted with the construction of the embankment to the

Chesterfield Road Bridge. For several years HUMMY's front end was stiffened by stout struts bolted to the end of the frames and the smoke box sides. Small shields were fitted over the front spectacles, and the original short cab roof was extended over the bunker after a few years' running; later a wooden back sheet to the cab was fitted. HUMMY was out of use at Clay Cross in 1946, taken out of book stock in 1950, and cut up on 1st June 1951 by Marple & Gillott Limited of Sheffield. One of the nameplates is displayed in the Narrow Gauge Museum at Towyn, Merionethshire.

GUY (first)—named after Capt. Guy Rolf Jackson, Derbyshire County Cricket Club skipper from 1922 to 1930 and the present joint managing director of the Clay Cross Company; fitted with brass nameplates measuring 18 in. by $7\frac{1}{4}$ in. with $5\frac{1}{2}$ in. letters on a red background. This was the second engine to be overhauled and had a short cab roof, but neither frame stiffening struts nor front spectacle shields were fitted. GUY was dismantled and then one Friday the frame and wheels were taken over to Fallgate on a Clay Cross Company Foden steam lorry normally used for transporting limestone. Next day the boiler and tanks were delivered and the engine was then reassembled by fitters Whiston and Grassick to work construction trains. When the railway was completed GUY needed a new tubeplate and other repairs but these were considered too expensive. One of the two locomotives which had just arrived from Thos. W. Ward Limited received the nameplates, and GUY never again ventured outside Clay Cross carriage shed, being cannibalised from time to time to repair the other engines. The remains were officially scrapped in 1939, and by 1942 only the corroded firebox remained in Clay Cross yard.

A visitor to the A.L.R. in August 1925 contends that this particular engine was named "Georgie" (after "Hummy" Jackson's wife, Georgina), and enthusiasts have subsequently referred to it as such. But the staff are quite adamant that, although two GEORGIE nameplates were actually cast, *they were never carried by the engine*. The plates were later sent over to Clay Cross Works when there was talk of them being put on an engine at the Company's Grin Quarries, near Buxton, but this did not take place and one was used as a shelf in the Works Loco Shed for many years.

JOAN—fitted with brass nameplates measuring 19 in. by 7 in. with letters $5\frac{3}{4}$ in. high on a red background. The third engine to be overhauled, JOAN was then dismantled and taken by road to Clay Lane; after reassembly by fitters Whiston and Grassick she was used on construction work in both directions. JOAN returned to Clay Cross when the railway was completed to be painted Midland "red" in readiness for working the first passenger train on 6th April 1925; this livery lasted until 1930 when it became plain black. Front spectacle shields and frame stiffening struts were fitted as on HUMMY, and the cab had a short roof which was subsequently lengthened (probably about 1947) to cover the bunker. JOAN ran for some time with a shorter stovepipe chimney than the others as a result of corrosion; a new chimney was not obtained but instead the rotted base portion was removed and the old one reused. About 1940 a skeleton frame was fitted between the rear of the cab roof and the bunker to carry a tarpaulin which gave better weather protection. In 1948 the left-hand tank developed a leak and, as the replacement from BRIDGET retained its nameplate, she was JOAN on the right but BRIDGET on the left! JOAN was not a popular engine, having a stiff regulator and being rather rough riding, so that it was not altogether surprising to see her out of use at Clay Cross late in 1948, although she was not officially taken out of stock until 1950. Various parts were removed to keep PEGGY running, and the remains were finally cut up on 24th May 1951 by Marple & Gillott Limited of Sheffield.

PEGGY—fitted with brass nameplates measuring 23 in. by 7 in. with letters $5\frac{3}{4}$ in. high on a red, later green, background. She was the last of the original four engines to be overhauled and worked as spare to HUMMY during the construction of the railway from Clay Cross. After this was completed she acquired a Midland "red" livery and hauled the second passenger train out of Clay Cross on 6th April 1925. PEGGY had frame stiffening struts as on HUMMY but not the front spectacle shields. About 1928 the left-hand cylinder fractured and, as the frames were in poor condition also, replacements were obtained from the first GUY. During this reconstruction PEGGY lost her stiffening struts and was also repainted unlined black. Her old frames lay around for some time before being cut up, and the cab was stored in the carriage shed with the remainder of the first GUY. In 1943 the boiler was replaced by the one off the second GUY, and at the same time the short cab roof was extended over the bunker. Driver Skinner made a cab *back*—sheet from the *front* of the second GUY's cab and this made things more comfortable for the crew when running bunker first out to Ford. By late 1948 PEGGY was the only steam locomotive in working order, thanks largely to the acquisition of a renewed boiler from BRIDGET and various parts from JOAN. She worked what was probably the last steam train when part of the track between Chesterfield Road and Hilltop was reballasted on 5th July 1949. PEGGY was taken out of stock in 1950 and cut up on 10th June 1951 by Marple & Gillott Limited of Sheffield. One of the nameplates is displayed in the Narrow Gauge Museum at Towyn, Merionethshire.

BRIDGET—fitted with brass nameplates measuring 16½ in. by 4 in. with 3 in. letters on a red, later green, background. She differed slightly from the original four in having a full length cab roof all the time, and a different type of live steam injector with wheel instead of lever control. Frame stiffening struts and front spectacle shields were fitted. She was a comfortable engine to ride on, but not quite so powerful as the others. A wooden back-sheet to the cab with circular spectacles was fitted in 1942 but three years later BRIDGET was out of use, although not withdrawn from stock until 1947. Her left-hand tank went on JOAN, and in August 1948 PEGGY obtained the boiler. The remainder was cut up in Clay Cross yard on 22nd May 1951 by Marple & Gillott Limited of Sheffield.

GUY (second)—it was intended to name this engine "Tommy"* and had this been done it is probable that the TOMMY plates would have come from the De Winton "coffee pot" locomotive at the Cliff limestone quarries at Crich. Instead the nameplates were transferred from the first GUY which was lying out of use when this engine, identical with BRIDGET, was received in good order from Thos. W. Ward Limited. GUY was acknowledged the best steamer on the railway but its sprained frames—the result of a derailment at Milltown— made it somewhat a rough rider. A short while before 1936 a back-sheet was fitted to the cab. The livery was always Midland "red", although latterly it appeared to be black owing to the thick coating of grime. GUY was not used after 1936 and by May 1939 was quite derelict at Clay Cross. In 1940 it was dismantled to provide spare parts but was not officially "scrapped" until the boiler found its way on to PEGGY in 1943. One of the pannier tanks had been requisitioned in 1940 by Clay Cross Works and incorporated in the hydraulic system of testing for the mortar bombs then being manufactured in the foundry (close to the gasworks). Twenty years later the tank was brought down from the roof of the building and the nameplate rescued for preservation

*Tom, General Jackson's eldest son, was killed in action at Arras on 9th April 1917; rather tragically this was his father's birthday. His parents visited the grave in France each year on this day, and in 1925 this meant leaving Clay Cross directly the A.L.R. opening day celebrations were over.

in the Company's offices. It is a matter of regret to the Company
Chairman that one of "his" HUMMY plates could not be obtained for
display alongside it.

(b) PETROL AND DIESEL LOCOMOTIVES

Many Light Railway Orders prohibited electric traction and
decreed that "the motive power shall be steam or such other motive
power as the Minister of Transport may approve." In this respect
the A.L.R. Orders were no different, but before long the "other motive
power" appeared on the scene in the shape of a four-wheel chain-driven
Fordson petrol locomotive; it had no cab and was painted grey. For a
few days in 1927 the makers demonstrated its ability to shunt three or
four loaded wagons at Clay Cross, but the A.L.R. was not impressed.
When not in use it stood in the carriage shed but, after it had narrowly
escaped damage from a string of wagons taking the wrong road from the
loop, the makers came along and removed it.

In actual fact this Fordson was not the first internal combustion
vehicle on the railway, this doubtful honour falling on five small four-
wheel inspection trolleys which were purchased for £20 each in 1925
(although not taken into stock until 1926). Each had a single-cylinder
two-stroke air-cooled petrol engine which was started by giving the
trolley a push and then jumping aboard when the engine fired; a "stick"
on a hinge-pin acted as a brake. Manager May and ganger Skinner had
one each and the others were spare; all five were scrapped about 1928.

At the end of the First World War, several (probably at least ten)
four-wheel petrol-electric locomotives had been purchased by the Clay
Cross Company from the War Stores Disposals Board, not for use as
locomotives, but because it was realised that the electric motors would
be very suitable as stationary haulage engines at the Company's
collieries. Like the Baldwins they had also seen service on the 60 cm.
gauge in France during the War, being built by Dick, Kerr & Company
Limited, Preston (W.D. nos. 1901* to 2000—louvred bonnet sides)
and British Westinghouse Electric & Manufacturing Company Limited,
Manchester (W.D. nos. 2001 to 2100—"panelled" bonnet sides).
Examples of both types were acquired by the Clay Cross Company.

*Nasmyth, Wilson & Company Limited, Manchester, actually *assembled*
the first three of the Dick, Kerr batch and probably provided parts for the
others.

Weighing 7 tons 7 cwts. empty, the width was 5 ft. 6 in., height 8 ft. 8 in., wheelbase 5 ft. 6 in., and length over frames 13 ft. 6 in. The builders used their own electrical equipment with a standard 40 h.p. petrol engine by W. H. Dorman & Company Limited of Stafford. This drove a generator which powered two traction motors so arranged that in the event of a breakdown the locomotive could work home on only one motor.

Sets of frames and wheels lay around for some years, while several of the cabs were used as telephone huts on the A.L.R. Then, about 1927, four more of these locomotives were purchased by the Clay Cross Company, two being primarily for spare parts. It was decided that one (by Dick, Kerr) should be overhauled and set to work in competition with the Baldwins to see which was the better. Taking the road in 1928, it was used for some two years as yard shunter at Clay Cross and also as an assistant engine on eight-wagon stone trains—banking from Hurst Lane or piloting from Ford Loop—after running out light engine from Clay Cross. No real challenge to the Baldwins was provided and when the daily passenger service ceased in October 1931 it had a short spell working the evening empty wagon train to Ashover, returning next morning with the "milk". An over-thirsty appetite for petrol when working hard boosted operational costs, and in 1934 it was placed in store in Clay Cross shed. There it languished until reinstated in 1937 to shunt Fallgate yard, with occasional journeys to Butts to collect materials or equipment. About 1937 one Ron Taylor chalked AMOS on the radiator front and as Amos Hind, the quarry manager, didn't seem to mind driver Banner went over the name in white paint and it became permanent. Towards the end of 1946 AMOS went over to Clay Cross Works for conversion to standard gauge, and was then despatched in November 1947 to the Company's ironstone pits at Bloxham, near Banbury. When these closed down in May 1954 it was used on tracklifting by scrap merchants Marple & Gillott Limited and then disposed of the same year to W. Bush & Son Limited, iron and steel merchants.

AMOS was removed to Helmdon but, before further use, suffered the evisceration of its uneconomic petrol engine which was replaced by a more suitable Gardner 4LW diesel. It assisted with tracklifting on the closed British Railways branch line between Cockley Brake Junction and Towcester (1954–1955), and then came three similar jobs—Midhurst to Petersfield (1956–1957), Hexham Junction to Riccarton Junction (1959–1961) and Greetland to Stainland (1961–

1962). In October 1962 the author came across a rather battered AMOS at North Cave when the former Hull & Barnsley Railway main line was being lifted between Little Weighton and North Eastrington (1962–1963). However, this was its last outing; the electrical equipment was worn out and AMOS was scrapped in May 1964 at Bush's Birchwood depot, Alfreton—not seven miles from Clay Cross.

As the condition of the Baldwins gradually deteriorated the need for another locomotive to work stone traffic became apparent. And so in 1939 Clay Cross Works coupled up a new three-cylinder McLaren diesel engine to certain resurrected parts of one of the four petrol-electric locomotives obtained about 1927. The cab controller indicated a 27 h.p. rating at 500 volts d.c., but this was misleading as the locomotive was more powerful than AMOS and 55 h.p. would be a more correct estimate. By using a diesel engine it had been hoped to run this locomotive more cheaply than AMOS but, although it held the road better than the Baldwins, the armatures often burned out and there were many teething troubles during the first few years' operation. It differed from AMOS in that the bonnet and cab were new; the latter could be entered from either side and not just from the rear. The front spectacles were extremely small, but the rear ones—rumoured to have been portholes recovered from the old "Majestic" liner—were much larger and more the usual size. On its trial run on 9th August 1939 the cab was found to be too high to clear the bridge in Clay Cross yard, and the track had to be lowered some 6 in. in consequence. The McLaren's top speed was no more than 6 m.p.h. with a load, yet it worked stone trains turn and turn about with the steam locomotives until April 1943 when it was put into store in the carriage shed. There it remained until taking over the duties of AMOS at Fallgate in 1946. When the electricity supply at Overton Quarry was changed over from d.c. to a.c. in February 1950 the McLaren was fitted up in Fallgate yard as a stationary power generator to power the spar washer, remaining in this guise until July the same year when it went to Clay Cross Works. The intention was for it to be rebuilt to standard gauge for Bloxham ironstone pits so as to replace AMOS, but this did not come about. After lying for some time in the Coney Green sidings at Clay Cross it was scrapped about 1957 by W. Bush & Son Limited of Alfreton.

Muir-Hill petrol locomotive no. 106, built by E. Boydell & Company Limited, Trafford Park, Manchester, was purchased about 1940 for shunting duties at Fallgate, but it was very rarely used. In appearance it resembled a Fordson farm tractor on a small four-wheel truck with outside bearings; a large gear wheel on the tractor's rear axle engaged with a smaller gear wheel on the front truck axle. It is understood to have been scrapped about 1945 but this cannot be confirmed. In fact the whole history of this locomotive is cloaked with uncertainty.

For the final eighteen months existence of the railway almost all the trains were hauled by a small 48 h.p. "Planet" diesel locomotive, built by F. C. Hibberd & Company Limited, Park Royal, London (works number 3307) and despatched new to Clay Cross on 16th July 1948. The leading dimensions were:

Overall width: 3 ft. 10 in.	*Wheel diameter:* 1 ft. 6 in.
Overall height: 7 ft. 7 in.	*Wheelbase:* 3 ft. 9 in.
Overall length: 12 ft. 1 in.	*Weight:* 6½ tons.

The speed range in m.p.h. at engine speeds of from 650 to 1,400 r.p.m., the tractive effort in lbs., and the maximum haulage capacity in tons on level track were:

1st gear: 1.73 to 3.74 (2,970 lbs.) 142 tons.
2nd gear: 2.88 to 6.18 (2,300 lbs.) 110 tons.
3rd gear: 4.73 to 10.02 (1,435 lbs.) 66½ tons.

The Vulcan-Sinclair fluid flywheel incorporated as a unit with the six-cylinder Perkins P.6 diesel engine was the first such application by the builders on a small "Planet" locomotive. An "anti-crash" type gearbox giving three speeds forward and reverse was controlled by a handwheel and no clutch was required. The axles were coupled by chains, and both hand and air brakes operated on all four wheels. Electric lamps were fitted to the front and rear of the cab, and the locomotive was painted green with white lining. This brought a little colour to the railway for both Amos and the McLaren had been a rather drab black. After the A.L.R. closed in March 1950 the "Planet" remained at Fallgate as yard shunter until disposed of by road in May 1951 to George Cohen, Sons & Company Limited. It was subsequently resold to R. G. Odell Limited and on 23rd June 1953 delivered to their wharf on Canvey Island in the Thames estuary where it was still in use in 1964.

A horse and a mechanical shovel took turns at shunting Fallgate yard for a month or two during 1951 until the arrival of a second-hand replacement for the "Planet". This was a small, cabless, and rather ugly four-wheel diesel (Ransomes & Rapier Limited, Ipswich, D.L. No. 82). Although re-engined in 1961, it was retired two years later. The present 48 h.p. four-wheel diesel (Ruston & Hornsby Limited,

Lincoln, no. 437367) boasts a full cab with lockable door, and arrived at Fallgate on 1st May 1963 after less than a hundred hours "field trials" at the pits of Hoveringham Gravels Limited, near Nottingham. It is the prototype of the Ruston standard Mark LF range of locomotives and has hydrostatic transmission as the "Dowty Transamatic Drive" plate on the cabside bears witness.

(c) CARRIAGES

Four saloon carriages, numbered 1 to 4 and lettered "ASHOVER LIGHT RAILWAY", were built in 1924 by the Gloucester Railway Carriage & Wagon Company Limited, Gloucester, for a total cost of £1,634 delivered to Clay Cross. New underframes and bodies of pitch pine and English oak with red deal sheeting had been constructed on centre-buffer trucks from old War Department bogie wagons supplied on embodiment loan by the A.L.R. A single bulkhead, with sliding door, divided the saloon between the second and third windows, and tramway type longitudinal perforated wooden seats covered with birch veneer provided seating accommodation for forty people. There was also a tip-up seat for three passengers at each end, but for statistical returns the A.L.R. reckoned the total capacity as only forty-two. The tramway illusion was carried a stage further by the provision of leather hand-straps on two rails running the length of the ceiling. On either side were six windows with drop lights, and at each end on both sides a sliding door with upper drop light and lower fixed light. Vacuum brakes were fitted and each carriage had at one end a gauge and an emergency application valve, all this equipment being supplied by the Consolidated Brake & Engineering Company Limited. Two drop lights were fitted at each end so that the conductor could operate the handbrake from within the carriage. Electricity for four interior lamps was supplied from accumulators kept under the seat at one end corner. An appropriate exterior livery of Midland "red" with gold lettering and lining was selected, and the interiors were painted cream. The *Railway Gazette* considered them to be "among the best to be found on railways of a light character, being clean, comfortable, and attractive interiorly."

Colonel Mount suggested that "having regard to the provision of rail level platforms it would be advisable to widen out the bottom steps to the extent of three or four inches. This would facilitate passengers stepping off the cars." Slightly bending the step supports had the desired effect! Two exterior lamp brackets—one on each side at opposite corners—were fitted at Clay Cross but only one oil lamp, showing a red aspect to the rear, was carried. The fitting of steam heating pipes under the seats was the only other alteration; knuckle-and-joint flexible copper connections to the locomotive proved unsuccessful and were replaced by lengths of rubber hose.

The four Gloucester carriages were insufficient to cater for the crowds of passengers in 1925 and two makeshift vehicles, piped for the vacuum brake, were converted from wagons. Transverse wooden seats (with arm-rests) were bolted to the floor and the wagon sides removed. An n-shaped support at each end carried a canvas canopy which was lashed to the supports and each seat-back by strong rope. In 1926 these vehicles reverted to wagons as by then additional carriages had been purchased.

An observer at Clay Cross seeing the delivery of eight carriages lettered "NEVERSTOP RAILWAY" might well have been forgiven for wondering just where these vehicles had worked, for the rubber shod wheels had no flanges! However, had he visited the British Empire Exhibition at Wembley in 1924 and 1925 he might well have travelled in them for there they operated on an unusual double-track line 3,300 ft. in length which ran from the L.N.E.R. Exhibition Station to Wembley Park on the Metropolitan Railway. Concrete strips set to a gauge of 2 ft. 10½ in. formed the running "rails" and, by installing special turntables at each end of the line, the track was made continuous. Motive power was provided by the "Adkins-Lewis Rapid Varying Speed Continuous Transport System", in which a spirally threaded shaft laid between the rails was rotated at constant speed by electric motors situated at convenient intervals. An arm attached to the carriage underframe carried a pair of rollers which engaged with each side of the spiral thread, and carriages travelled faster when the pitch of the thread was coarse and slower when it was fine. By varying the pitch at points along the screw the speed of the carriages was also varied, so that they almost came to rest in stations and accelerated and slowed down uniformly between them. Because of the unconventional "rails" at Wembley it was necessary to fit each carriage with a small horizontal guide wheel at right angles to each carrying wheel. Among the advantages claimed for the "Neverstop" system were impossibility of collisions, quick acceleration, and the ability to surmount steep gradients and sharp curves. It was devised by Wm. Yorath Lewis, M.I.MECH.E.,

A.M.I.E.E., and a short experimental line was built about 1911 in the vicinity of Ipswich. A similar system to that at Wembley, but with much smaller carriages, had been built for the Amusements Park at Southend-on-Sea in 1923. Swansea Corporation considered the "Neverstop" for its Town Hall estate and the system was discussed in Berne (Switzerland) and Valparaiso (Chile), but the obvious disadvantages seem to have outweighed against any commercial application.

Lewis ordered his equipment for the Wembley system from the Drewry Car Company Limited in 1923, with the proviso that the builders should retain no drawing or photograph. Construction of the carriages was actually carried out in the main by a subsidiary company, E. E. Baguley Limited of Burton-on-Trent, with the remainder sub-contracted out to Richard Garrett & Sons Limited of Leiston, Suffolk. Of the ninety-seven gaily painted carriages, eight were purchased by the A.L.R. in 1926 (although not taken into stock until 1927). The bodies, which were not altered in any way, were completely open along one side apart from the five roof supports; no guard chains were fitted. Wood panels without doors formed the lower half of the other side and wire netting covered the remainder, glass being used only in the three end windows. Three pairs of back-to-back transverse slatted wooden benches, set in slightly on the open side and with no intermediate partitions, gave seating accommodation for twenty-four and at the same time left plenty of room for standing passengers.

At Clay Cross Works the steel frames and bogies were removed and replaced by wooden frames mounted on centre-buffer trucks from old W.D. bogie wagons. Handbrakes were fitted at each end but, as the carriages were only piped for the vacuum brake, they were officially permitted to run only next to the engine or between a pair of Gloucester carriages. Steam heating and electric lighting were not provided for there was no intention of using them in the winter. Before going into service (one or two in 1926 and the remainder in 1927) they were painted Midland "red", lettered "ASHOVER LIGHT RAILWAY" and numbered 5 to 12 but, unlike the Gloucester carriages, were not lined out. Known as "monkey carriages", "streamliners", "charas" or "open-air carriages", at busy periods all eight would be in traffic. Generally speaking holidaymakers liked them, for excellent views of the countryside could be obtained with plenty of fresh air into the bargain. However, storage in the open at Ford Loop during the winter, because there was no room for them in the carriage shed, soon led to a deterioration in their condition.

For the meagre winter traffic it was thought that a small bogie carriage would be sufficient as this would enable an extra wagon to be worked each trip. Specially designed frames were built, but the body was not assembled and parts remained for many years in the carriage shed. Some sections were eventually used during the War when a canteen was constructed for Italian prisoners working at the Slag Plant in Clay Cross Works. In 1946 one carriage side (*length:* 13 ft. 6 in.; *height:* 6 ft. 8 in.) with nine windows was "recovered" from the disused canteen by foreman-fitter Fred Piper and with other pieces of "scrounged" timber used to make a fitters' cabin at the Slag Plant; it was still in use in 1964.

A conductor travelled on each train issuing tickets in exchange for cash fares. He attended to the oiling and cleaning of carriages daily, and was also responsible for lighting station lamps at dusk and extinguishing them when the last train called; the crossing gates at Stretton and Woolley were locked overnight and undone by the conductor when reached by the first train of the day. At busy times a second conductor assisted on all trains from Clay Cross during the morning, returning to the terminus from the station where the up and down trains crossed. During the late afternoon and evening he would work the Ashover end of the line to cope with the crowds returning home. It did occasionally happen, on Sunday afternoons for instance, that not all passengers could be booked before Ashover, so packed were the trains.

In September 1936 the Wembley carriages went out to Ford Loop for storage as usual but, being needed no more, there they remained until returning to Clay Cross in 1942. By now in a most dilapidated condition they continued to decay still further and, when some additional siding space was required about 1944, their doom was sealed. The bogies were recovered for use as wagon spares, but the bodies were unceremoniously smashed up and burned.

Protected in the carriage shed from the ravages of time, the Gloucester carriages were in a fit condition to see further service during the War period inside Clay Cross Works. Two (No. 1 and No. 2) became storesheds near the fitting shop and the others a women's canteen (later storesheds) near the gasworks. After the official opening of the new sportsfield at Clay Cross on 24th May 1952 someone had the bright idea of bringing out these old carriages. No. 4, painted dark green with cream window frames, appeared first in 1953 alongside the bowling green and was fitted up with an awning along one side. In

July the following year the other three carriages were set up as "stands" by the football pitch. Individual fold-up chairs replaced the longitudinal seats, while the rear sides were boarded up and the window frames and glass removed from the front. When the cricket pitch boundary was extended in 1960 one of the carriages had to be set back, but it was in such a poor condition that there was no option but to scrap it. One of the others was blown over during a gale in February 1961, and both needed repairs.

Among those who saw the carriages on the sportsfield were representatives of the Lincolnshire Coast Light Railway at Humberston, near Cleethorpes, which was opened to traffic on 27th August 1960. Negotiations for the sale of the two "stands" were successful and they were removed to Humberston during 1961, the first on 8th July and the second on 22nd July. Seven double and seven single reversible seats from scrapped Glasgow "Green Goddess" and "Cunarder" tramcars were fitted and, using old W.D. wagon bogies obtained from the defunct Nocton Estate light railway near Lincoln of Smith's Potato Estates Limited, one of the carriages went into service on 20th April 1962 and the other followed on 2nd November 1963. In 1964 the seating was slightly altered and one of the carriages appeared in a new exterior livery of light blue and cream. The earlier L.C.L.R. dark red livery was not far removed from the original A.L.R. finish.

At Clay Cross carriage No. 4 was moved to an adjacent side of the bowling green about 1958, losing its acquired awning in the process but, even though the ventilators and lamps have been removed and the bulkhead centred in the saloon, it remains a most vivid reminder of the palmier days of the Ashover Light Railway.

(d) WAGONS

Fifty bogie open wagons with wooden bodies, purchased with certain spares for £2,392/8/– from the War Stores Disposals Board at about the same time as the first four locomotives, were stacked three or four high alongside the standard gauge goods line near the L.M.S.R. tunnel mouth until required for construction work. A further twenty, costing £450, arrived in 1925 from Thos. W. Ward Limited, the Sheffield dealers. They were given numbers between 1 and 70 which were painted on the sides in small white numerals; "A.L.R." also appeared in large white shaded characters, and the overall livery was a light grey. Built in large quantities during the 1914–1918 War by such firms as Cravens Limited (Sheffield), Gloucester Railway Carriage & Wagon Company Limited (Gloucester), Robert Hudson Limited (Leeds), and G. R. Turner Limited (Langley Mill, Notts.), the wagons were of standard War Department designs on either steel or wooden frames. Each bogie truck was fitted with a centre buffer and the handbrake shaft was operated by a handle or wheel. On the majority of the wagons the whole of each side of the body unpinned in two parts (W.D. class "D"), but on some only the centre section could be dropped. The latter body was that fitted to the W.D. class "E" wagon which had truss bars of a type that fouled the tippler at Clay Cross and prevented easy tipping of stone. Although soon equipped with replacement class "D" truss bars these wagons were not popular for they were difficult to unload *anyway*. Just how many were purchased originally is not known, but for a good few years only four (53, 55, 57 and 69) were in use. Another difficulty when wagons were tipped was that oil ran freely from the axleboxes. Conversion to grease resulted in anything but easy running and at the start of a run it was necessary to go round with an oilcan to loosen them up.

Two wagons became temporary passenger vehicles in 1925 (see previous sub-chapter), and slight modifications to another enabled it to carry a large 9-ton tar tank. This was filled from a standard gauge oil tank wagon standing on the bridge which carried the standard gauge dirt tip line over the narrow gauge track into Clay Cross Works. Tar was conveyed to Milltown as required, which was at least twice a week and sometimes daily. A smaller 6-ton tar tank, mounted on the bogie chassis specially built for the small carriage (see previous sub-chapter), was held in reserve. Other small tar tanks, transferred to the narrow gauge from standard gauge wagons outside the Khartoum Foundry, were worked to the limestone tarmacadam plant in Clay Cross Works. After a few years and one or two cases of locomotives getting out of control on the steep gradient down to the Foundry, rope haulage was substituted; the same electric winch which pulled A.L.R. wagons on to the tippler was employed.

In an endeavour to do away with transhipment of coal which tended to break up large lumps intended for domestic sale at Fallgate and Ashover, a bogie transporter wagon (L.M.S.R. 195312) was purchased in 1934 from the 2 ft. 6 in. gauge Leek & Manifold Valley Light Railway (closed 10th March 1934). Built in 1904 by Cravens Railway Carriage & Wagon Company Limited of Sheffield, it was a most unusual vehicle for this country. The leading dimensions were:

Length: 19 ft. 6 in.   *Bogie Wheelbase:* 4 ft. 3 in.
Width: 8 ft. 0 in.   *Centres of Bogies:* 9 ft. 0 in.
Wheels: 1 ft. 9 in.   *Tare Weight:* 4¾ tons.

To alter the gauge one wheel was pressed off each axle-shaft which was then turned up in the lathe at Clay Cross Works, the surplus length removed, and the wheel pressed in the required distance. At the same time the vacuum brake piping was taken off and the handbrake gear slightly altered. A trial run up the line with a standard gauge wagon aboard showed that on straight sections the transporter ran quite smoothly, but when negotiating sharp curves the wheels fouled the bogie frames and the *tout ensemble* threatened to topple over. This failing and also its heavy loaded weight of some twenty tons resulted in a veto on its further use by the Consulting Engineer. It may be thought that the eight standard gauge wagon bodies forming the Butts Quarry storage hoppers were taken up on the transporter, but in actual fact they were conveyed on narrow gauge wagons without sides and ends. The transporter itself was banished to Ford Loop with the Wembley carriages and stayed there until removed about 1942 to Clay Cross yard. There it rapidly became very derelict, but its rusty remains were not cut up until 1951.

It is interesting to note that consideration had been given to a transporter in the early days of the railway. "I will speak to you re 'conveyor' for M. L. trucks," wrote Colonel Stephens on 6th November 1922, but what he said to General Jackson resulted in the matter being dropped. A vehicle which would probably have seen about as much use as the transporter was brought to the General's notice in August 1924. This was a practically new crane with a span of 10 ft. 10 in. carried on two 2 ft. gauge bogies, which was offered at Barry for £195 by The Bute Works Supply Company Limited. Colonel Stephens was quite enthusiastic. "You will never get a better bargain. I wish I could alter it to 2 ft. 4 in. gauge. I would have it for my Snailbeach line." But the General could see no real need for it on *his* railway and made only a small offer which the Bute Company politely declined.

On 31st March 1925 when Colonel Mount inspected the A.L.R. there were "forty-six ten-ton bogie wagons in use", and this suggests that four of the original fifty had been dismantled to provide bogies for the Gloucester carriages. The grand total of wagons on the A.L.R. never exceeded seventy and as only twenty were purchased from Thos. W. Ward Limited it would appear that some of the spares later became wagons. That the Ward wagons were obtained in 1925 there is no

doubt, yet the Annual Returns show that they were not brought into
stock until later. The Returns segregate the wagons into 8-tonners and
10-tonners but do not differentiate between steel and wooden frames.
The latter are *stated* to have been 8-tonners, but it is not thought
that there were ever as many as twenty *wooden* frame 8-tonners on
the A.L.R.; several were in fact rebuilt with new frames of steel channel-
ling. As built the wooden frame wagons had four-plank body sides
with a tare weight of $2\frac{1}{2}$ tons, and could carry a load of $9\frac{1}{2}$ tons; the
steel frame wagons were respectively three-plank, 2 tons 15 cwts. 1 qr.,
and 10 tons. Allowing for a gap in statistical information from 1940 to
1946 the stock totals at each year end were:

> 8-*tonners:*   1925 (nil), 1926 (19), 1927–1931 (20), 1932 (19), 1933–1935
> (18), 1936–1937 (17*), 1938 (16), 1939 (14), 1940–1946 (?),
> 1947–1948 (8), 1949 (5).
> *One was "sold" to the Clay Cross Company's Grin Quarries
> in 1936.
> 10-*tonners:*   1925–1939 (50), 1940–46 (?), 1947–1949 (47).

In March 1950 there were still fifty-nine *apparently* serviceable
wagons but within a year about thirty were broken up. Parts of one or
two were sold and used to make some pig huts near Chesterfield Road
station, and two others were dumped at the bottom end of Fallgate
yard near the spar washer. The latter were purchased about November
1962 by the Midland Group of the Festiniog Railway Society, and the
bogies went to Portmadoc as spares. The bodies and underframes were
not required, but two couplings were used in the construction of
Festiniog Railway brakevan No. 1 which was completed in 1964.

Twenty-one wagons (renumbered in a fresh series from 1 to 12
and 14 to 22) still remained at Fallgate in 1964, and the dozen or so in
use between the washing plant and the fluor spar storage bunker
appeared to be in quite good condition; they were all of the steel frame
variety with full length drop sides. Some sported new planking but
several sagging sides still displayed the fond initials "A.L.R."

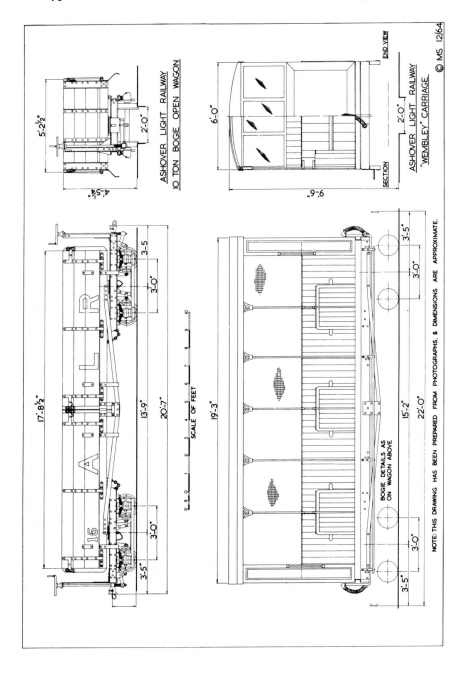

ASHOVER LIGHT RAILWAY
10 TON BOGIE OPEN WAGON

END VIEW

ASHOVER LIGHT RAILWAY
"WEMBLEY" CARRIAGE

SECTION

© MS 12/64

SCALE OF FEET

BOGIE DETAILS AS ON WAGON ABOVE

NOTE: THIS DRAWING HAS BEEN PREPARED FROM PHOTOGRAPHS. & DIMENSIONS ARE APPROXIMATE.

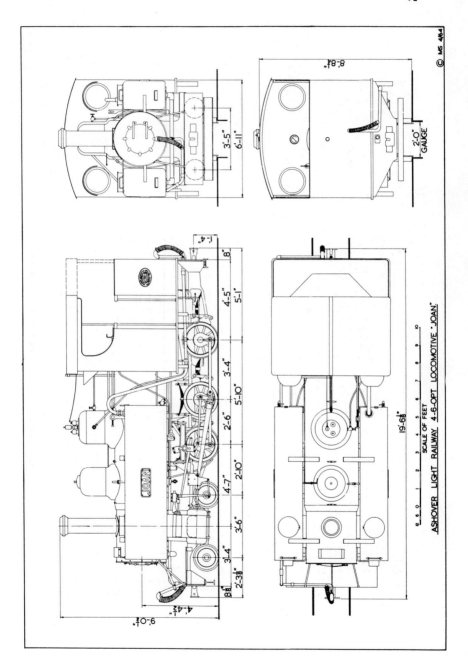

ASHOVER LIGHT RAILWAY 4-6-0PT LOCOMOTIVE "JOAN"

SCALE OF FEET

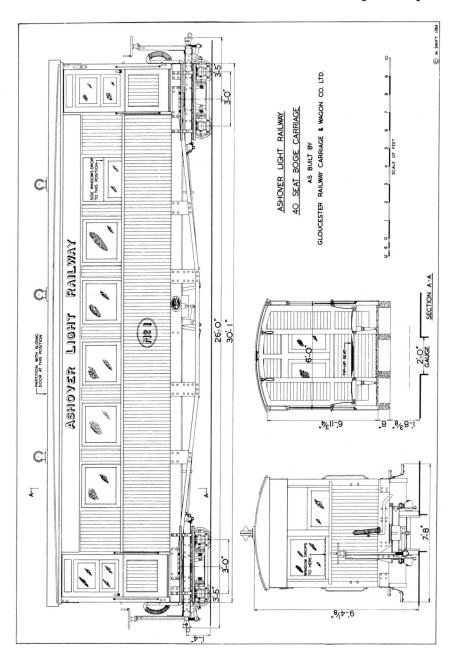

ASHOVER LIGHT RAILWAY
40 SEAT BOGIE CARRIAGE
AS BUILT BY
GLOUCESTER RAILWAY CARRIAGE & WAGON CO. LTD.

SCALE OF FEET

SECTION A-A

© M. SWIFT 1/84

9—DISSOLUTION

Having "died" to all intents and purposes fourteen years previously, the complete closure of the A.L.R. on 31st March 1950 passed by unnoticed in the Press. Not until publishing an advertisement concerning the liquidation of the Company in its issue of 18th August 1950 did the local *Derbyshire Times* make any mention in its news columns. As the railway had slumbered most of the day for several years a casual visitor would have noticed few changes, but even so the Butts pre-cast concrete plant shed and "Rainbow" cafe had by then been removed to Clay Cross where the former was in use at the Works as a garage. All the track within Butts Quarry had been removed shortly after its closure but in August 1950 the main line was still *in situ*. It was not complete as 24 ft. lengths of track had been removed at Clay Lane, Stretton and Woolley, a large log of timber blocked the rails between Stretton and Clay Lane, whilst Hilltop Loop was completely isolated with barbed wire stretched across each end. The section between Fallgate and the Milltown spar washer remained in use with wagons shunted by the "Planet" diesel which made its last run to Butts on Saturday, 21st October 1950, to collect various items of equipment.

On Monday, 23rd October 1950, the three lengths of track were replaced and the obstructions removed so that the "Planet" could work through to Clay Cross. There it collected a wagon with seats, and for the last time worked a scheduled trip to Fallgate. H. H. Jackson (Clay Cross Company Chairman), R. F. Childs (Clay Cross Company Estate Agent) and F. J. Rooth (solicitor, of Blakesley and Rooth, Chesterfield) were the passengers on this historic journey which had been arranged so that an inspection could be made of the strip of land available for sale (the last portion was sold in March 1955) once the track was lifted. As the land beyond Milltown was entirely Clay Cross Company property (part of the Overton Estate) the special did not work through to Ashover and the passengers returned to Clay Cross by car. One notes with interest that the first and the last A.L.R. trains to carry passengers were both official specials, and that on each occasion wagons were used and not carriages.

Marple & Gillott Limited of Sheffield commenced tracklifting on the same day as the last train, and by January 1951 had cleared the section between Clay Cross and Stretton. Rails and sleepers were stacked in Woolley yard, but Fallgate was the base of the contractors' small four-wheel "Planet" diesel locomotive. Previously owned by G. Cohen Sons & Company Limited (plant number HS 2922), it broke down soon after arrival and many of the demolition trains were worked by the A.L.R. "Planet". Almost all the track in Clay Cross yard was taken up during the last week in February, by which time the station buildings at Ashover had been demolished and only the line between Fallgate and a point beyond Ford remained. By mid-May the track south of Milltown spar washer had been lifted, and scrapping of the steam locomotives was under way.

All bridges except the one between Hurst Lane and Woolley, where the trackbed was in use as a footpath, were removed by W. Twigg (Matlock) Limited. With the demolition of Chesterfield Road bridge towards the end of September 1951 went the most vivid reminder to passers-by, for it had displayed on either side since 1931 an advertisement for "Pirelli" tyres. Clay Cross & Egstow station building, in use for some time as a workshop by the Clay Cross Works diesel engine fitter, had been moved over to the Clay Cross sportsfield in June 1951 and with minor modifications became a cricket pavilion; the fitter continued his work in the former Butts concrete plant shed at Clay Cross Works. In 1952 part of the carriage shed was removed to the Slag Plant where it was still in use in 1964 as a garage for dumper trucks. After the locomotive shed had been dismantled Clay Cross yard stood empty and deserted, but it was used again as a coke stocking ground from about 1955 until the Clay Cross blast furnaces closed down in 1958.

A writer in the 1929 Year Book of the East Derbyshire Field Club remarked that only a moderately sized dam near Ogston Hall would convert the lower part of the Amber valley into a lake, and on 5th March 1954 the North East Derbyshire Joint Water Committee voted to do just this. The cost of the scheme, which had been under consideration since the previous August, was estimated at over £860,000. Great concern was aroused and many protests were made, but construction of the dam wall on the Ashover side of Ford Lane was commenced in June 1955 by Lehane, Mackenzie and Shand Limited. Impounding of water started in October 1957, and when completed in June 1959 Ogston Reservoir covered over 200 acres and held some 1,300 million gallons. It has flooded the A.L.R. from Ford to some distance beyond Woolley, and a pipeline to the Wingerworth coal carbonisation plant of the National Coal Board—officially opened by the Minister of Fuel and Power on 30th October 1956, and prime user of the water—runs on or near the trackbed from Ford Lane to Hilltop cutting.

So much of the railway has been desecrated that a visit to the surviving section at Fallgate now generates a feeling of nostalgia. Memories of happier times crowd the mind . . . We are at the lineside. The Amber ripples peacefully, but the air is still. A whistle echoes along the valley. And then the last train to Butts is upon us, headlamp wavering, the exhaust loud and clear. We are shrouded in steam. Was it PEGGY? Or JOAN? . . . The vision fades. Its like we shall see no more. For the Ashover Light Railway has gone for ever.

Some A.L.R. tickets in the Author's collection.

APPENDIX A

Chronology

11.1918	Application for powers to construct a standard gauge railway from Stretton to Ashover with a 2 ft. gauge branch railway to Alton Colliery.
4.12.1919	The "Ashover Light Railway Order 1919" confirmed.
11.1921	Application for the standard gauge railway to be built to 2 ft. gauge and extended to Clay Cross.
9.1922	First sods lifted at Fallgate.
13.11.1922	"The Ashover Light Railway (Extension &c) Order 1922" confirmed.
Spring 1924	Railway opened to goods traffic from Clay Cross to Fallgate.
5.1924	Application for extensions in Ashover to Butts Chapel and Amber Lane.
26.8.1924	"The Ashover Light Railway (Extension) Order 1924' confirmed.
31.3.1925	Inspection of the railway by Colonel Mount on behalf of the Minister of Transport.
6.4.1925	Official opening of the railway.
7.4.1925	Public passenger service commenced.
3.10.1931	Daily passenger service ceased.
25.3.1932	Passenger service reintroduced on a limited scale only.
13.9.1936	Passenger service suspended.
8.6.1940	Last public excursion train.
24.8.1947	Last passenger train (special).
28.1.1950	Butts Quarry closed.
2.3.1950	Final meeting of the Ashover Light Railway Company.
31.3.1950	Railway closed to all traffic.
20.5.1950	Winding up Order issued by the Minister of Transport.
26.7.1950	Ashover Light Railway Company liquidator appointed.
23.10.1950	Last train (official special from Clay Cross to Fallgate).
5.1951	Tracklifting completed (apart from the retained sidings at Fallgate).

APPENDIX B

Stations, Distances and Altitudes

m. chs.	altitude*		m. chs.	altitude*	
0 00.00	385	Clay Cross & Egstow	5 38.09	427	Dale Bank
			5 61.00	441	Milltown
0 38.00	445	Chesterfield Road	6 02.74	456	Fallgate
			6 18.00	474	Power House Siding
1 14.47	417	Holmgate			
1 32.60 (a)	411	Springfield	6 54.72	502	Salter Lane
1 51.75	404	Clay Lane	7 05.28	527	Ashover (c)
2 44.37	362	Stretton	7 24.20 (d)	555	Butts Quarry
3 55.49	332	Ford Siding	7 10.27	537	Ashover (e)
4 09.60	348	Hurst Lane	7 14.21 (b)	540	Ashover (Butts)
4 52.73 (b)	386	Woolley			

NOTES— *height in feet above sea level.
  (a) estimated distance.
  (b) nòt 4 52.75 and 7 13.70 as previously published.
  (c) southern point of triangle.
  (d) estimated distance to end of track.
  (e) northern point of triangle.

CLAY CROSS & EGSTOW, CHESTERFIELD ROAD, STRETTON, FALLGATE and ASHOVER (BUTTS) were classed as stations, the remainder halts.

The Annual Statistical Returns showed 39 chains of "second track" (i.e. loops) and 1 mile 6 chains of sidings.

Cast-iron mileposts were erected at ¼-mile intervals from zero at CLAY CROSS & EGSTOW. Yet Clay Cross to Ashover was "up"!

APPENDIX C

ESTIMATE OF EXPENSE – RAILWAY NO. 4

		£	£
1. Preliminary expenses			250
2. Construction costs:			
Cuttings—excavation of 22,000 cubic yards of soft soil at 3s. 6d. per cubic yard . . .		3,850	
One bridge over public road		1,600	
Accommodation Bridges and Works . .		600	
Culverts and Drains		900	
Metalling of Roads and Level Crossings . .		100	
Permanent Way, including Fencing—2m. 6f. 5c. at £1,600 per mile		4,500	
Permanent Way for sidings and cost of junctions .		2,000	
Stations and Buildings		1,000	
Plant including signalling and telegraphic apparatus		800	
Contingencies at 10 per cent.		1,535	
		16,885	16,885
3. Land and Buildings to be acquired . . .			1,600
4. Rolling Stock			5,000
5. General Charges			500
6. Interest on capital during construction . .			1,500
7. Sundries			3,000
Total amount to be charged to capital . .			28,735

(This estimate, which is representative of others prepared for the A.L.R. by Colonel Stephens, was submitted to the Ministry of Transport in November 1921 when powers were sought to construct *Railway No. 4*. No figures are available to allow comparison with the actual costs.)

APPENDIX D

A.L.R. CAPITAL ACCOUNT FROM THE COMMENCEMENT TO 31ST DECEMBER 1925

	£	s.	d.
Wages and Salaries	14,887	8	5
Construction Materials and General Equipment . .	4,602	15	7
Land purchased (*excluding* Overton Estate) . .	4,059	19	6
Rails and Fishplates	3,877	4	1
Legal and Professional Charges	3,496	10	4
Wagons (70)	2,842	8	0
Carriages (4)	1,634	0	0
Locomotives (6)	1,600	0	0
Sleepers	1,108	3	11
Commission of Colonel Stephens	1,000	0	0
Coal	694	11	10
Transport and Delivery Charges	672	15	5
Insurance	556	11	4
Spares and Equipment (Locomotives and Rolling Stock)	488	12	6
Chesterfield Road bridge erection	358	10	0
Printing and Advertising	159	5	8
Bridges (16)	155	0	0
Inspection Trolleys (5)	100	0	0
Train Staffs	64	10	0
Crossing Gates	44	6	0
Compensation to Farmers	40	13	0
Tickets	30	11	6
Miscellaneous Expenditure (*including* several items for Alton Colliery)	1,503	6	9
	43,977	3	10
Less items in stock and other "credits" . . .	3,059	13	11
Total Capital Expenditure	40,917	9	11

APPENDIX E

TRAFFIC AND RECEIPTS

	Passenger Trains		Traffic		Receipts		Net
	S	W	Goods (tons)	Passengers	Goods £	Passengers £	Revenue £
1925	8(5)	7(3)	17,860	63,657	1,464	1,079	— 843
1926	5(4)	5(4)	44,198	35,063	3,416	640	+ 391
1927	8(5)	5(–)	65,958	29,794	5,072	603	+ 406
1928	5(2)	5(–)	55,433	32,529	3,948	464	+ 371
1929	5(2)	4(–)	48,002	25,118	3,488	397	+ 542
1930	5(3)	4(–)	42,617	23,384	2,867	361	+ 19
1931	5(3)	—	41,880	17,044	2,942	219	+ 654
1932	6(3)	—	34,235	16,484	2,366	197	+ 32
1933	6(3)	—	28,305	18,265	2,011	255	+ 62
1934	6(3)	—	33,292	15,116	2,208	185	+ 101
1935	6(3)	—	33,840	16,872	2,356	184	+ 39
1936	6(3)	—	33,561	11,686	2,368	139	+ 7
1937	—	—	31,906	*	2,132	10	+ 65
1938	—	—	22,532	—	1,618	—	— 238
1939	—	—	*	—	1,331	—	— 160
1940	—	—	*	*	908	6	— 419
1941	—	—	*	—	825	—	— 688
1942	—	—	*	—	2,870	—	+ 269
1943	—	—	*	*	1,201	6	— 617
1944	—	—	*	*	1,774	6	— 36
1945	—	—	*	*	1,616	6	— 122
1946	—	—	*	*	1,730	6	— 194
1947	—	—	14,034	88	1,398	9	—1,927
1948	—	—	16,089	—	1,671	—	—2,014
1949	—	—	14,550	—	1,522	—	— 885
1950	—	—	*	—	182	—	— 342

*Information not available.

S   Summer Service   W   Winter Service

Passenger Trains

There was a certain amount of variation in the summer when extra trains ran only on certain days of the week. The tables show the number of advertised trains which operated *daily* during the peak period, the Sunday totals being given in brackets. From 1932 to 1936 trains ran only during the summer months on three days a week, and after 1936 only special trains were operated.

Traffic (Goods)

Minerals (i.e. limestone and fluor spar) constituted over 90% of this traffic. Coal was the only other major item (7% in 1925 although normally no more than about 4%) but this dwindled from a maximum of 2,429 tons in 1926 to 21 in 1947, the last year it was carried. Individual tonnages in 1928 were: limestone 49,830; fluor spar 3,198; coal and coke 1,907; milk 251; manure 150; general goods 85; grain 10; timber 2 (total 55,433 tons). Some of the "merchandise" was carried by passenger train, and in 1928 this swelled the passenger receipts by £71 (with £83 included in the goods receipts).

Traffic (Passengers)

Six years' receipts from workmen totalled only £61 17s. 0d., the numbers carried being 2,964 in 1925, 3,072 (1926), 1,524 (1927), 312 (1928), 456 (1929) and 408 (1930).

Train Mileage

The total mileage attained a maximum of 38,036 in 1927, but then showed a steady decline as the following figures show.

1925 — 3,670 Passenger; 21,708 Mixed; 126 Goods; and 769 Shunting
       (includes also banking and piloting).
1931 — 1,875 P; 4,848 M; 11,514 G; and 649 S.
1936 — 1,400 P; 2,610 M; 9,945 G; and 175 S. (Last year of mixed trains.)
1949 — 5,672 G; and 250 S. (Steam accounted for only 616 G and 20 S.)

APPENDIX F

Authorised Train Loadings in 1925

Clay Cross to Hilltop
    2 coaches plus 2 loaded wagons, or
    2 coaches plus 5 empty wagons, or
    4 loaded wagons.

Hilltop to Ashover
    2 coaches plus 4 loaded wagons, or
    2 coaches plus 10 empty wagons, or
    6 loaded wagons.

Ashover to Ford
    2 coaches plus 7 loaded wagons, or
    2 coaches plus 10 empty wagons, or
    10 loaded wagons.

Ford to Clay Cross
    2 coaches plus 4 loaded wagons, or
    2 coaches plus 7 empty wagons, or
    5 loaded wagons.

(One coach was equal to one loaded or two empty wagons.)

APPENDIX G

TICKETS AND FARES

Tickets issued (and punched) on the train by the conductor were of the thin Bell Punch type (2½ in. by 1¼ in.) similar to those in use at the time on most bus and tramway undertakings, but 12-journey workmen's and free passes were Edmondson type thick card tickets (57 mm. by 31 mm.). Seasons could be obtained in advance from Clay Cross station but were not very popular. Workmen's tickets produced a little more revenue but, with the suspension of the daily passenger service in 1930, they were discontinued. The reverse side of the Bell Punch tickets carried various A.L.R. advertisements such as "Coal, Lime and General Merchandise carried at reasonable rates", "Organised Excursion Parties not exceeding 100 at reduced fares" and "Send your milk and farm produce by the railway; you will find it cheaper".

For a short time in 1925 excess fare receipts were issued to children instead of ordinary tickets, and this was standard practice always for bicycles, dogs and perambulators. In 1935 a combined bus, train and tea ticket was introduced, in conjunction with The Ellis Travel Bureau Limited of Chesterfield, for the journey to Chesterfield Road station by Corporation bus, thence A.L.R. to Ashover, and finally a plain tea at the cafe there. Although of an experimental nature the scheme was well patronised both by individuals and parties, and proved so successful that it was operated again in 1936.

It is interesting to note that tickets printed in March 1925 were still being issued on the last day of passenger services. The known examples are listed below.

Thin Card Tickets

1d.	single	(white)	6d.	return			(light green)
1½d.	,,	(dark blue)	6d.	cheap day return			(purple)
2d.	,,	(light blue)	7d.	,,	,,	,,	(mid-green)
3d.	,,	(red)	8d.	,,	,,	,,	(khaki)
4d.	,,	(pink)	9d.	,,	,,	,,	(greyish brown)
5d.	,,	(mid-green)	10d.	,,	,,	,,	(yellow)
6d.	,,	(khaki)	1/–	,,	,,	,,	(lilac)
7d.	,,	(light green)					
8d.	,,	(yellow)					
9d.	,,	(red)					
10d.	,,	(lilac)*					

*10d. single A11 0000, the first ticket to be issued from Ashover to Clay Cross on 7th April 1925, is preserved at the Clay Cross Company offices.

Pasteboard Tickets

2s. 6d.	Workman's	CW 1 Clay Cross – Ashover (buff)
1s. 9d.	,,	CW 2 Clay Cross – Hurst Lane (purple)
1s. 0d.	,,	CW 3 Clay Cross – Clay Lane (light brown)
—?—	,,	CW 4 —?— – —?—
6d.	,,	CW 5 Milltown – Ashover (dark green)
—	Free	E/FT (buff)

The maximum rates laid down by the 1919 Order for passengers were 3d. per mile (1st Class), 2d. per mile (2nd Class) and 1d. per mile (3rd Class). Charges for small parcels varied from 3d. (up to 7 lbs.) to 9d. (14 to 28 lbs.), but for "any parcel exceeding fifty-six pounds but not exceeding five hundred pounds in weight the Company may demand any sum they think fit". These rates and charges, however, were repealed by the 1922 Order which laid down that "the Company may make charges not exceeding those demanded . . . by the Midland Company" or its successor.

The original cheap return fare from Clay Cross to Ashover was 10d., but from 31st May 1925 this was increased to a shilling, the single fare remaining at 10d. By 1930 the day return fare had dropped to 9d., and in 1932 6d. was all that was asked for the fifteen mile return journey. Value for money indeed! Children under three years of age were carried free with half-fares (minimum 1d.) for those over 3 but under 12.

The fare table dated 30th April 1925 for Cheap Return Tickets on Wednesdays, Saturdays and Sundays is reproduced below.

Clay Cross & Egstow
```
Clay Cross & Egstow
 –   Chesterfield Road
 –   –  Holmgate
 3   –   –  Springfield
 3   –   –   –  Clay Lane
 4   4   3   3   3  Stretton
 7   7   6   6   5   3  Hurst Lane
 8   8   6   6   5   4   –  Woolley
 8   8   8   8   6   4   3   3  Dale Bank
 8   8   8   8   6   4   3   3   –  Milltown
10  10   9   9   8   6   3   3   –   –  Fallgate
10  10   9   9   8   6   5   3   3   –   –  Salter Lane
10  10   9   9   8   6   5   3   3   3   3   –  Ashover (Butts)
```

APPENDIX H

EMPLOYEES

Although I have listed all A.L.R. employees whose names are known to me it is quite probable that a few are missing. Statistics reveal that in 1935 there were nine "operatives", one female clerk and a manager, but ten years later the entire A.L.R. labour force totalled four—J. Banner, C. Maycock, E. Skinner and H. Skinner.

Managers
Capt. John May (1924–1927), George Harry Wilbraham (1927–1940).

For several years the post of Manager was styled "Secretary and Manager"; officially the Clay Cross Company Secretary was also the A.L.R. Company Secretary, but routine matters were dealt with at the office on Clay Cross & Egstow station. A certain John May was Traffic Manager on the Londonderry & Lough Swilly Railway during the period 1912–1916, but it is not known whether this was the A.L.R. John May. By about 1922 the A.L.R. John May appears to have been assistant manager of the Festiniog Railway (probably on the commercial side). Not long afterwards he became Traffic Superintendent of the Festiniog and Welsh Highland Railways for a short time, and quite probably came to the A.L.R. on the recommendation of Colonel Stephens who was Engineer to all three railways. When May found that A.L.R. repairs executed at Clay Cross Works were being costed rather high he sought leave to have them done elsewhere, but General Jackson asked his departmental managers to reduce their prices and so help the A.L.R. pay its way. This did nothing to promote friendly relations for May was intensely proud of his little railway and wished to develop it in his own way. It seems that there was a final difference of opinion which resulted in May's resignation and return to Wales. The A.L.R. staff were genuinely sorry to see him go for he was from all accounts a most capable manager, of friendly disposition, and highly respected.

Originally a draughtsman, Harry Wilbraham had served the Clay Cross Company in several executive positions before taking over as A.L.R. Manager. After a lengthy spell of sickness, when into his seventies, he died in 1940. Shortly before his death, responsibility for the Clay Cross end of the line (i.e. locomotives mainly) had been delegated to the Clay Cross Works slag plant manager (John Dunn) and for the Ashover end (i.e. traffic mainly) to the Butts and Milltown

Quarries manager (Amos Hind; George Towndrow from 1944). There was no definite point of division of the railway, and when difficulties arose around Stretton and Ford they were resolved by mutual co-operation.

Consulting Engineers

Holman Fred Stephens (1918–1931), William H. Austen (1932–1940).

Stephens is mentioned in the text of Chapters 3 to 6. Shortly after his death on 30th November 1931, Austen, his former assistant, asked whether the A.L.R. wished inspections to continue. At a Company Meeting on 18th April 1932 it was agreed that Austen should become Consulting Engineer on the same terms and conditions as Stephens, "the fee being at the rate of £25 per annum plus an allowance of £25 per annum for expenses, the appointment to date from 1st April 1932 and to be determinable by three months notice on either side."

Inspections were carried out twice a year, and Austen would walk as far as Stretton with manager Wilbraham (or ganger Skinner) before riding through to Ashover in a carriage attached to the rear of an empty stone train. After lunch they would walk back to Stretton where the coach would be awaiting them in the loop; it was coupled up to the first stone train through to Clay Cross.

From 1941 to 1950 the position of Consulting Engineer was vacant.

Engine Drivers

J. W. "Bill" Banner, Reg Ling, Harry Revell, Harold T. Skinner, John Stevenson, Bill Taylor, George Whitworth.

Revell and Stevenson were the first two drivers on the A.L.R., the latter being known as "Staveley Jack" following his earlier employment at the Staveley Ironworks. Revell fell ill after the opening day and did not resume, being replaced by Ling, a standard gauge locomotive driver at Clay Cross Works, during the summers of 1925 and 1926. Taylor drove GUY at Fallgate during construction work, but left the A.L.R. before 1925. Banner started as a platelayer in 1923 and succeeded George Symonds as fireman in mid-April 1925 at a rate of a shilling an hour; became a driver—generally with the second GUY—in 1927 at 1s. 3d. an hour; ceased "main line" driving in 1936 and thereafter drove AMOS and worked for the Clay Cross Company at Milltown until retiring in September 1963. Skinner started at Clay Cross Works in 1925, transferred to the A.L.R. on Whit Monday in 1926 and was fireman to Bill Banner for several years; became a relief driver in 1927 and a regular driver nine years later; resigned in April 1940 but returned in 1942 to drive PEGGY *only* while the opencast site was in operation; in the event he stayed on and did not finally leave until April 1947. Whitworth, previously a 'bus driver, had the McLaren locomotive for a short period in the 1940's.

Firemen

Billy Johnson, George Symonds, Billy Towndrow

Symonds and Towndrow were with the A.L.R. before 1925 and fired for Stevenson and Revell respectively. Towndrow was JOAN's fireman on the opening day but left later in the month; Symonds followed not long afterwards. Johnson started as a wagon repairer and became a fireman about 1926.

Conductors

Billy "Picker" Allen, Charlie Maycock, Bert Robinson

Allen and Robinson were the original conductors, but the latter left in 1929 after working for a while as a platelayer with his brother Tommy. Allen also repaired wagons, drove AMOS a little about 1930, and later fired for Skinner before eventually transferring to Clay Cross Works. Maycock held the unique record of being the only person to be with the A.L.R. from start to finish; he commenced in 1923 on construction work and was then wagon repairer/relief conductor, fireman, and latterly driver of the "Planet" locomotive.

The train crews in 1927 were—driver Banner, fireman Skinner, conductor Allen; and Stevenson, Johnson and Robinson. The conductors normally changed trains weeks about.

Fitters

Jack Grassick, George Mills, Jim Moreland

Grassick started with the Clay Cross Company in 1913 and assisted with the overhaul of the Baldwin locomotives when purchased. In 1924 he moved over to the A.L.R. as foreman fitter in charge of steam locomotive repairs, and generally managed to get in two afternoons' driving each week also, as well as helping out at holiday times. He watched over the running of the A.L.R. while manager Wilbraham was off sick, and left in 1940 when maintenance work was transferred to the Clay Cross Works Loco Department and fitter Tom Whiston. (AMOS and the McLaren locomotive were always the responsibility of the "electric shop" fitters at Clay Cross Works.)

Fitter's Mates

Maurice Skinner (1930–1939), Dennis Symonds (1925–1930), Arthur Wheeler (1926–1928).

Symonds was also a spare fireman—often with spare driver Grassick. Skinner also acted as a spare driver.

Coach and Wagon Repairer
Henry Tomlinson.

Gangers, Platelayers and Lengthmen
Fred Barker, Jack G. Martin, Harry Nixon, Amos Quemby, Tommy Robinson, George Short, Edward "Teddy" Skinner, Ernest Slinn, Jim Walvin.

In August 1924 Colonel Stephens persuaded Skinner to leave his job as ganger on the West Sussex Railway and get the A.L.R. permanent way in order for the opening. He was appointed foreman ganger in 1925, and originally (changes were made several times subsequently) was responsible for the section from milepost 1¼ to Ashover. Short, previously in the Clay Cross Works gang, looked after the remainder, assisted by Walvin; in the early days these two also handled all transhipment to standard gauge wagons until this duty was passed over to the Clay Cross Works tarmac department. A drastic reduction in permanent way staff found Skinner with only two plate-layers in 1936; almost unbelievably four years later he had none at all! Until retiring in December 1945 he was assisted on minor track repairs by the train crew, but for big relaying jobs the Clay Cross Works gang was called in. (Skinner's two sons were also employed on the A.L.R.)

From January 1926 to January 1937 Martin lived in the only piece of property owned by the A.L.R. (other than the "Rainbow" cafe) which stood to the west of the line just north of Stretton level crossing. During wet weather Horsecar House was liable to be flooded and because it was not unknown for livestock to be taken upstairs at these times the local people knew it as "Pond Hall Farm"! The cottage was demolished in 1937.

Clerks
Ethel Foster, Betty Jones, Elizabeth Walvin.

At busy periods Walvin took turns of duty as a conductress.

APPENDIX I

The Ashover Light Railway Company

The "Ashover Light Railway Order 1919" provided that "Thomas Hughes Jackson and Brigadier-General Geoffrey Meinertzhagen Jackson and John Steen and all other persons and corporations who have already subscribed to or shall hereafter become proprietors in the undertaking . . . are hereby incorporated by the name 'The Ashover Light Railway Company' ". The capital of the Company was £62,000 in 6,200 shares of £10 each, of which any portion not exceeding £31,000 could be issued as preference capital, while borrowing was restricted to a sum not exceeding £31,000. The 1922 and 1924 Orders decreased the authorised capital to £48,000 and £51,000 respectively, and proportionately amended the preference capital as well as the amounts which could be borrowed. Expenditure on the capital account was met temporarily by the Clay Cross Company, no capital being issued until 6th December 1928 when it was resolved "that 5,100 shares of £10 each fully paid up be allotted to the Clay Cross Company Limited, pursuant to agreement dated 14th March 1928."

During the Company's life span T. H. Jackson, G. M. Jackson, R. O. Jackson, H. H. Jackson, G. R. Jackson, H. A. Sanders and J. W. T. Holland served for varying periods as Directors, and J. Steen, W. H. Lee and A. R. Parsons were successive Secretaries. (These persons were also respectively Directors and Secretaries of the Clay Cross Company.) T. H. Jackson (died 3rd January 1930) was succeeded as Chairman by his son, G. M. Jackson (died 9th September 1946) and finally by his grandson, H. H. Jackson.

The earliest entry in the Minute Book refers to an extraordinary meeting on 23rd January 1922 prior to the submission to the Minister of Transport of the Draft Order for *Railway No.* 4, and subsequent minutes for the most part deal with the sealing of deeds of land purchased by the Company. At the final meeting held on 2nd March 1950 it was "resolved that Arnold Robert Parsons, acting Secretary of the Ashover Light Railway Company be appointed Secretary of the said Company and that he be directed to apply to the Minister of Transport for an Order under Section 7 of the Light Railways Act 1912 that the Ashover Light Railway Company be wound up and that Henry Humphrey Jackson be authorised to make a Statutory Declaration in support of such application". This was duly sworn before R. E. Hill, a Commissioner for Oaths, on 17th July 1950, after the issue of a winding up Order by the Minister of Transport on 20th May 1950.

The final act was played out before Mr. Justice Vaisey in the Chancery. Division of the High Court of Justice and on 26th July 1950 Tom Alistair Macfarlane of 83 Cotton Exchange Buildings, Old Hall Street, Liverpool, was appointed liquidator of the Ashover Light Railway Company.

THE ASHOVER LIGHT RAILWAY

CORRIGENDA AND BRIEF ADDENDA

page 7, para 4   The full name of General Jackson, referred to here *et passim*, was Geoffrey Meinertzhagen Jackson (see page 86). The family home was Clay Cross Hall, not far from Clay Cross & Egstow station.

page 16, footnote   I am told that the steam navvy still lay derelict in 1936.

page 22, line 17   *Before* "Dolly" *Insert* Dorothy

page 25, para 2   The *Railway Gazette* report of the possibility of mineral traffic being worked by gravity was no doubt referring to the abortive *Railway No.2* to Alton Colliery which would have been far too steeply graded to have been worked by locomotives.

page 26, para 4   *The third sentence should read:* A locomotive (thought to be GUY) was once hit by a runaway lorry in Fallgate Yard and toppled over; JOAN was derailed near Dale Bank with a loaded stone train after hitting an obstruction on the track; and on another occasion there was a near collision at Holmgate with a horse and cart.

page 26, line 36   The 30th May 1930 was a Friday, not a Thursday.

page 32, para 3   The Railway Executive cancelled the two existing contracts for basalt ballast and chippings by a letter dated 11th January 1950. However, this had been requested by the Clay Cross Company on 21st December because "the Stonebreaking and Screening Plant at our Ashover Quarries and the Ashover Light Railway . . . have completely worn out".

page 33, footnote   *Add:* Goods facilities were withdrawn from this station by British Railways with effect from Monday, 4th May 1964. The last passenger trains called on Saturday, 31st December 1966, and the station buildings and platforms were subsequently demolished.

page 34, line 12   Clay Cross Company's *should read* L.M.S.R.

page 45, footnote   Stubben Edge Hall was taken over in August 1921 and opened as a convalescent home on 20th July 1922.

page 49, para 1   John May did not select the name for the cafe. Miss Joan Jackson has told me that some years previously the Jackson family had greatly enjoyed a play staged in

Liverpool and entitled "Where the Rainbow Ends". The basic design of the cafe was roughed out on the back of an envelope by General Jackson, and from this the working drawings were made.

page 50, para 1   The wooden tubs in use latterly at Butts Quarry replaced the earlier V-shaped steel double-side tipping wagons.

page 50, para 2   It is understood that the first four Baldwins might have come from the War Department depot at Chilwell, near Nottingham, rather than from Darlington.

page 51, last para   The boiler length of the Baldwin locomotives was 6 ft. 11 in., the overall length of the complete locomotive being 19 ft. 6⅛ in. The grate area was 5.6 sq. ft.

page 54, para 3   The building date of BRIDGET, according to Baldwin worksplate 44737, was 1.1.1917. Note that *all* the letters on the nameplates of BRIDGET (and the other locomotives) were of *equal* size, and not as printed throughout the book.

page 57, para 2   BRIDGET was named after General Jackson's youngest daughter.

page 58, para 2   It has been suggested that the Fordson may have been another Muir-Hill locomotive (similar to the one purchased in 1940) in view of the fact that Muir-Hill used "Fordson" components.

page 61, para 2   The "Planet" diesel was ordered on 11th February 1948, according to the maker's records, and the 'Delivery Date' is quoted as 15th July 1948. R. G. Odell Limited sold it about October 1972 from their Canvey Island site for preservation at the East Anglian Tramway Museum at Carlton Colville, near Lowestoft. However, since about July 1981 it has been on the Festiniog Railway in North Wales.

page 61, last para   The Ransomes & Rapier loco was ordered on 2nd February 1938 by Rotherham Sand & Gravel Company Limited, and supplied new to them at Scrooby, near Retford, Notts. It originally had a 20 h.p. Ailsa Craig engine and weighed 2½ tons. Although withdrawn from service in 1963, it lingered on at Fallgate until 1969 when it disappeared, presumably disposed of for scrap.

page 62, para 1   The Ruston & Hornsby locomotive, a 7 ton machine, left the maker's works new on 24th April 1959. It ceased work at Fallgate in 1968 and remained there until 1970 when it was moved to Clay Cross Works for storage in the open. About October 1971 Alan Bloom, of Bressingham Hall, near Diss, Norfolk, acquired it for preservation, but on 27th November 1980 it moved to the Bromyard & Linton Light Railway at Bromyard, near Hereford.

page 63, line 17 "NEVERSTOP RAILWAY" *should read* NEVER-STOP RAILWAY.

page 69, para 1 The 1944/45 edition of *The Universal Directory of Railway Officials and Railway Year Book* (published in 1944) shows a reduction of 9 in the total wagon stock from the previous year. However, it should be noted that the stock totals given in previous editions of this publication (and its predecessor, the *Railway Year Book*) are not always in agreement with the A.L.R.'s Annual Returns!

page 74, para 1 The small green "Planet" locomotive, *operated* by Marple & Gillott Limited, carried the painted number 402 on the right hand side of the bonnet cover above two plates—"HS 2922" and "Property of George Cohen Sons & Co., Ltd., Stanningley Works, Stanningley, Nr. Leeds". On the other side of the bonnet it was lettered "H. E. Pitt Ltd., Sunderland". No builder's plates were carried, but this diminutive locomotive was one of a batch built by the Motor Rail & Tramcar Company Limited at Bedford for War Department Light Railways service during the 1914–18 War. Several were later purchased by F. C. Hibberd & Company Limited who replaced the petrol engines with diesels—a Gardner "National" in this instance—before resale. It is somewhat ironic that former War Department locomotives were used in both the construction, operation and demolition of the Ashover Light Railway.

page 75, line 6 The use of locomotives at Fallgate had ended by 1968, and the bogie wagons—by then in a very run-down condition—were shunted by a road vehicle. Rail traffic had ceased entirely by March 1969 and the surviving wagons were disposed of later that year.

page 81 In 1983 the Transport Ticket Society published an illustrated 42 page survey of the A.L.R.'s tickets, ticket practices, fare tables and passenger train services. Written by Glynn Waite and entitled *Tickets of the Ashover Light Railway*, it is highly recommended.

page 81, lines 7/8   *Amend to read:* a little more revenue, but were discontinued in 1930. The reverse side of the Bell

page 83, para 2   John May lived very close to Clay Cross Works at 23 John Street, Egstow.

INDEX

(The plate numbers of photographic illustrations are indicated in **bold type**.)